HOW TO TALK TENNIS

by Peter Schwed

Illustrated by Taylor Jones

Dembner Books • New York

Dembner Books
Published by Red Dembner Enterprises Corp., 80 Eighth Avenue, New York, N.Y. 10011
Distributed by W. W. Norton & Company, Inc., 500 Fifth Avenue, New York, N.Y. 10010

Library of Congress Cataloging in Publication Data

Schwed, Peter.
    How to talk tennis / Peter Schwed : illustrated by Taylor Jones.
       p.   cm.
    Includes index.
    ISBN 0-942637-01-1 (pbk.) : $8.95
    1. Tennis.   2. Tennis players—Biography.   I. Title.
GV995.S356   1988
796.342'092'2—dc 19
[B]   87-30604
                                      CIP

CONTENTS

INTRODUCTION

Tennis has been played at least as far back as the thirteenth, perhaps even the eleventh, century, but not the game we know. That didn't start until 1873 at a lawn party in Wales, where one Major Walter Clopton Wingfield introduced it as a new game he had invented. He called it Sphairistike, but many found it easier (and more amusing) to shorten that to "sticky." (Why Sphairistike in the first place? Well, he chose a word that goes back to ancient Greece and Rome, where it referred to a ball game and the room or enclosure in which it was played.) Soon the simpler, more descriptive name "lawn tennis" became popular, and that's what we call it today, even though few people play it on a lawn any more.

The medieval game, however, has first claim to the name. Because it was popular with royalty, and was played at the royal court, it was called "court tennis" and, sometimes, "royal tennis." (One of the interesting excursions that visitors to London can enjoy is a trip to the famous playing area enclosed in the body of Hampton Court Palace, down river on the Thames. That's one of the few chances most people can ever get to glimpse such a sight, and at least for the sports-minded, the sight is well worth a visit.) A court-tennis court is modeled upon the playing areas, along with their appurtenances, that were part of French monasteries and Italian piazzas, complete with covered gallery, a grille, and penthouse, and the complicated game grew out of what was played in those structures, built for other purposes. Obviously the construction of such a court is elaborate and very expensive, so the number of courts in the world, and the number of players, is limited. Still, for the sake of the record, *that* is the original game, but once having made acknowledgment of the fact, we would do well to forget it. Our interest is in what we all know now simply as tennis. (Even though it is still semantically "lawn tennis," the venerable United

States Lawn Tennis Association was realistic enough a few years ago to change its name to the United States Tennis Association. The growth of that game—our game—during the past twenty years has been so spectacular that it has been termed the Tennis Explosion.)

The first great championship—men's singles—was played at Wimbledon, in England, in 1877, four years after Major Wingfield's garden party, and, with the exception of the war years of World War I and II, has been held every year since. A women's championship, starting in 1884, has had the same history. The Wimbledon championships are regarded as the most prestigious of all tennis events, due to their history, tradition, and the fact that they are still contested on grass. Other court surfaces may be as good, or better, but grass is still considered a special and very precious heritage of the game.

The United States National championships, formerly also contested on grass but for the last decade played on hard-surface courts, hasn't the venerable aura of Wimbledon, but it is an equally important world competition tournament, and winning it means every bit as much as winning Wimbledon. Our National tournament was first held in 1881, for men, and in 1887 for women. It has been played every year since.

Another great national tournament has been the French, which is played on clay, and which began in 1891 for the men and 1897 for the women. The war years knocked out the French championships, as they did Wimbledon's. The final major tournament, which comprises the fourth tournament of what has become known as the Grand Slam, meaning a sweep of all four in one year, is the Australian. That championship didn't begin until 1905 with the men, and not until 1922 with the women. Since Australia is so far away, the travel requirements often discourage the best players from the West from making the journey, so the tournament doesn't have the same numbers of top-quality players in the draw as the other three tournaments, and this has lessened its stature in recent years. Still—if you want to achieve the Grand Slam, you'll have to travel to Australia and win their championship as well as the other three, all within one calendar year. Some great players, who might well have done that, never got around to it, and only two men and two women have managed the achievement.

For about the first two-thirds of this century, tennis was for the most part a game for the classes, rather than the masses. It was played in the United States on such lovely, social, rarefied courts as Newport, Southampton, Longwood, and Seagirt—all with grass courts and all leading up to the grand finale of the Nationals, also played on grass, at Forest Hills. In England, comparable summers saw preliminary tournaments played on grass at such sites as Hurlingham, Queens, Eastbourne, and culminating at Wimbledon. Costumes became more abbreviated, with mens' long white flannel trousers yielding to shorts, and women's long skirts to short ones, but the color was always the traditional white of tennis. The great tournaments were for amateurs only, and while professional tennis had been flourishing after a fashion ever since the mid-1920s, the only people who could make real money from it were the very best two or three in each era, who went on national tour. If you were, let us say, only the tenth best player in the world, there was no money in professional tennis for you. The result was that nobody turned professional except a great champion now and then, who could start a new tour against the old champion. For the rest, the rewards in tennis lay in amateur ranks, winning Wimbledon or Forest Hills, or being on the Davis Cup winning team, so the important world of tennis remained amateur. (Never mind that the word *shamateur* was coined to describe the "amateur" who received money by various under-the-table ploys offered by the promoters of various tournaments: that happened a lot. But tennis players did hold down regular jobs: there was no big living to be engineered out of amateur tennis.)

Professional tennis owes much to the late promoter Charles C. (Cash and Carry) Pyle, who in 1926 offered the great Suzanne Lenglen of France $50,000 to tour the United States. That was an idea that seemed outlandish, since tennis crowds and gate receipts had never been very big, but it was agreeable to Mlle. Lenglen. Pyle then signed up a topnotch American woman player, Mary K. Browne, to be a foil for La Belle Suzanne, and four men as well, including one of the best in the world, Vincent Richards, and three lesser but good players. The tour, which everybody except Pyle thought would be a catastrophic failure, turned out to be such a smashing success that, at

8 the end of it, Pyle gave Lenglen a $25,000 bonus, and all the rest of the players did very well by 1926 financial standards, with Pyle himself clearing $80,000.

After that, a professional organization was created, once again without much anticipation of success from many; but when, through the years, great champions like Bill Tilden, Ellsworth Vines, Don Budge, Bobby Riggs, Jack Kramer, Pancho Gonzales, and eventually the great Australians like Lew Hoad, Ken Rosewall, Ashley Cooper, and Rod Laver traded in their amateur laurels for professional cold cash, pessimistic proclamations ceased. Not too many professional players existed, for only the very best received offers to turn pro, but those who did made out very well.

The fly in the ointment for them was that they couldn't compete in the great tournaments, and newcomers whom they felt they could beat took the spotlight. Then in 1968 it all changed. All of the major tournaments became "open" championships, meaning that professionals were welcome to compete against amateurs. This meant that, for the first time in close to half a century, all of the world's best could match strokes against each other on the sacred grounds of Wimbledon and Forest Hills. Television saw a big opportunity and stepped in with big offers for extensive coverage, backed by commercial sponsors fighting for the privilege. The Tennis Explosion was on, and not just in world-class tournament circles.

Public enthusiasm for tennis, both watching it and playing it, erupted to an extent never visualized before. People of all sorts, of all ages and both sexes, who had never played before, took up the game. They joined clubs, took lessons, and purchased the flood of new (and expensive) tennis paraphernalia, including clothes that were rushed out and suddenly became fashion items whether one played the game well or not, or perhaps not at all. Expensive indoor facilities were built all over the country to allow year-round tennis. The National championships moved from the comfortable, charming, historic site of the West Side Tennis Club at Forest Hills to newly constructed highly commercialized quarters in a stadium constructed at Flushing Meadow, and with good reason. Tennis had become a big-time sport—it was no longer a social one. Forest Hills could only seat

14,000 spectators. Flushing Meadow not only could accommodate
three times that number, but financial geniuses came up with a
number of other angles. The price of tickets could, of course, be
marked up fantastically, with such a surge of interest in attending and
seeing the Nationals—or did many simply want to attend in order to
be seen there? The tournament could be broken up into two sessions
daily for all the days leading up to the semi-finals, thus obtaining two
admission charges per seat per day, rather than one. Blocks of tickets
for the semi-finals and finals could be sold to the companies that
sponsored the tournament and to other corporations that could afford
to purchase such expensive blocks for business purposes. The fact
today is that a normal, loyal fan who has been attending the Nationals
faithfully for decades finds it almost impossible to get in for either of
the two big days unless he has friends in powerful places in the
business community, or goes to a ticket speculator.

But not to worry. That normal, loyal fan will be able to see the semi-
finals and finals on national television, and admittedly see the play
rather better than from a mediocre seat in the stands. But there are
people who feel there's no substitute for *being there*! What do you
think?

As you may have gathered, tennis is a sport that lends itself to
differences of opinions and arguments, but they can be good arguments because there's usually much to be said for both sides of the
controversy. I may have more affection for old memories of attending
championships at Forest Hills than I do now at Flushing Meadow, but I
still have a lot of fun there, and heaven knows that the benefits to
tennis, and to tennis players, have been enormous in material terms. I
may suspect that my new graphite frame, which cost more than $100,
is wildly overpriced compared with my old wood racquet, and maybe
not better at all, but I still did buy it, and I might not be as happy
without it.

However, if you really want to see the fur fly in a tennis bull session,
steer the topic around to who was the best player of all time! It's
nonsense, of course, because the best that one can be is the best of
one's own time; comparisons between generations are futile. Conditions, and the character of the game, change too much from era to

era. There is only one sure concession to be made. Anyone asked to list the dozen greatest male players who ever lived is sure to include Big Bill Tilden without hesitation, which isn't absolutely true of any of the other greats. A person making such a selection might well believe that one or another of his choices would actually have beaten Tilden, and so wouldn't rank Tilden first, but no one would leave Tilden off such a list, whereas any of the others might be left off in favor of somebody else. I, for instance, in the listing that follows most reluctantly did not include another dozen, any of whom could be as valid candidates as many I did include. I might have bumped any of the others in favor of one of these, but not Tilden!

Does that make Bill Tilden the undisputed best of all time? More people would probably say that he was than would name anyone else, but as the song lyricist put it, it ain't necessarily so. It might be argued with justice that any of the dozen players who follow was the top male player the world has ever seen, but there's no way of proving anybody's contention. So let's just set up a list of candidates for such a mythical crown, along with their credentials, and let the arguments begin! (In order to avoid even a subliminal suggestion of favoritism in the order of listing, both this list, and the brief one of my alternate dozen that follows, are simply alphabetical.)

Donald Budge. The redhead left amateur ranks when he was only twenty-three, and in his last year as an amateur, 1938, he scored the only Grand Slam ever recorded in men's tennis up to that time. Budge's Davis Cup victory over Germany's Baron Gottfried von Cramm, in the previous year, is easily one of the most memorable matches every played.

Henri Cochet. France's Four Musketeers, who kept that country solidly in charge of the Davis Cup from 1927 through 1932, were all such brilliant players that any or all of them might make this list. However, Toto Brugnon was essentially a doubles star, so he doesn't. Cochet, who won Wimbledon twice and the U.S. National once, is considered by many the best of the group, but it's impossible to rank him ahead of René Lacoste, who appears on this list later, who also won Wimbledon twice and the U.S. championship twice as well. Jean Borotra, who regretfully didn't *quite* make this list (but did make the alternate list), could be more brilliant than either Cochet or Lacoste, and he won Wimbledon twice himself, but he wasn't as consistent as the other two.

Jimmy Connors. Connors won both the Wimbledon and U.S. titles in 1974, when he was turning twenty-two, did the same in 1982, when he was thirty, and during the intervening years was usually the finalist in one or the other or both tournaments as well. He was without question the outstanding player in the world over that stretch of time, yet people are more likely to remember him as the man you hate to love than for anything else. For Jimmy, who turned a lot of people off with his frequently vulgar and even obscene gestures and language (tempered considerably in recent years), won your love when you saw him battle on the court. No player ever had more heart, and no player ever came back so often from what seemed to be decisive defeat to win important matches. Now, having passed the age of thirty-five, which for most great players is considered a kind of graveyard age, he is still arguably the best American male player in the game.

Jack Crawford. Gentleman Jack was a giant among giants, playing in an era when Tilden, Cochet, Lacoste, Perry, and Vines were his rivals. He came close to sweeping the boards in his best year, 1933, when, after winning his native Australian championship, he beat Cochet for the French crown, toppled Ellsworth Vines to win Wimbledon, and only finally succumbed, in the U.S. National, to an inspired Fred Perry in the fifth set of a match, tiring at the end.

Richard Gonzales. Of all the great players, tennis came more naturally and with the least hard work to Pancho Gonzales, who said he never had to sacrifice or to work particularly hard, because it all was such great fun. It was only one year after he started playing against ranking players that he won the U.S. National—an unprecedented accomplishment. After he won that tournament again the following year, Gonzales turned professional and continued his brilliant career. It is interesting that he rated Lew Hoad (who is on my list of the alternate twelve) as "probably the best and toughest player when he wanted to be," and Francisco (Little Pancho) Segura as the most underrated player in the game.

Jack Kramer. There were many attacking players before Jake

Kramer, but none who consistently came in behind every serve. The big serve, combined with the big follow-up volley, became known as the Big Game, and it was Kramer who brought it into being and who, using it, simply was invincible as an amateur in 1946 and 1947, and later was the same in professional tennis.

René Lacoste. Great as Cochet and Borotra were, probably Lacoste was the best and most feared of France's Four Musketeers. It was Lacoste who played the biggest part in finally bringing to an end Big Bill Tilden's unchallenged six-year domination of the courts. Lacoste won the U.S. National championship in 1926 and 1927, and beat Tilden in the critical match to win the Davis Cup for France in 1927.

Rod Laver. Rocket Rod would probably garner more votes than any player other than Tilden in a popular election as to who was the greatest player of all time, and with good reason. For details, see the article about him.

Ivan Lendl. Lendl, who was born in Czechoslovakia in 1960, won every important junior championship in the world in 1978, and there didn't seem to be any doubt at all that this rather dour, silent eighteen-year-old would scale the heights of men's tennis very soon afterwards. And indeed he did, making his mark in tournaments all over the globe throughout 1980 and 1981, and finally achieving No. 1 ranking at the end of 1982. Although he has never renounced Czech citizenship and become an American, the way Martina Navratilova did, he has done the next thing to it and essentially lives in his home in Greenwich, Connecticut, and has become thoroughly American in habits and in speech. Not that he talks much, and this has hurt his image somewhat with those many United States fans who warm to players who are so articulate on and off the courts that they are positively brash. Lendl lets his racquet do the talking, and for the past half dozen years, the United States Open has been his particular pet platform. He has consistently performed wonderfully everywhere and on every surface, but he is the King of Flushing Meadow.

Fred Perry. During a four-year span (1933–1936), Perry won all eight of his Challenge Round singles matches as Great Britain won and held the Davis Cup against France, the United States, and Australia; he won three successive Wimbledons and three United

States singles titles, and for good measure one French and one Australian championship. It's doubtful if any one player ever compiled so impressive a record over an equal period of time, and it's no wonder that a statue of Perry stands, welcoming visitors, within the gates of Wimbledon.

William T. Tilden, II. See the article about Big Bill.

Ellsworth Vines. Everyone agrees that Vines at his best was unbeatable, and his best in amateur ranks came in 1931 and 1932, when he won the United States crown in both years, and the Wimbledon title in the second. Vines hit the ball harder than anyone the game has ever seen, but his style made him the victim of occasional serious slumps. He turned professional in 1934 and dominated pro circles for five years until Budge turned pro, but all who ever played Vines are unanimous that, at his best, Elly was the best.

There isn't a name among those dozen that couldn't lay pretty convincing claim to having been the best player the tennis world has ever seen, and without going into any detail about them, this second list includes several who well might have comparable claims: Bjorn Borg, Jean Borotra, Norman Brookes, H. L. Doherty, Roy Emerson, Lew Hoad, Billy Johnston, John McEnroe, John Newcombe, Bobby Riggs, Ken Rosewall, Frank Sedgman.

So start talking tennis! Let the arguments begin! Let the brickbats fly!

LEXICON

Ace ♠

Roscoe Tanner

n: a serve that the receiver not only is unable to return, but can't even tick with his racquet. Common usage sometimes abuses the term to include a serve that is so difficult to reach, and so severely hit, that the receiver only barely is able to touch it, and can't possibly return it. That's a great winning serve—yes—but it's not an ace.

advantage

n: (often shortened to "ad") the next point after a game has reached deuce. It will be either server's advantage (ad in) or receiver's (ad out). If the player who has the advantage wins the following point, he wins the game. If he loses it, the score reverts to deuce.

ad court

n: the left~hand half of the play~er's court, so called because when~ever the score has reached ad in or ad out, the serve must be delivered into the service box on that side.

alibi

Ilie Nastase

n: an excuse offered by a loser as the reason for his defeat. No sport

John
McEnroe

(alibi cont'd)

is immune, but tennis seems to have more than its share of alibiers. "The linesmen were blind," "Nobody can play in that wind," "I didn't get a wink of sleep last night," "My knee is still bothering me from that tumble I took a while back," "I raised a blister midway in the first set," and so forth, ad infinitum and ad nauseum. This virus never seems to have infected Australian or Swedish players, more credit to them.

all

adv: the tennis synonym for "each." When the score of a game reaches 15~15, for example, the umpire calls "Fifteen~all!"

alleys

n: the two rectangles, 4 feet 6 inches wide and 78 feet long, that border each side of a tennis court. In singles, they don't come into play at all, and are disregarded. They are very important in doubles, which is why they exist. Without having to cover that extra 9 feet of width, two good doubles partners could so dominate the net that it would be virtually impossible to pass them.

amateur

n: a player who does not play for money, or accept money as a result of his fame, as opposed to a professional. Today, as far as the best players in the world are concerned, amateurism has virtually ceased to exist. Since the monetary rewards in professional tennis are great, there's no point in remaining an amateur any longer, now that all the big tournaments are Opens—open to professionals as well as amateurs. Something nice has been lost as a result, but the gain of huge piles of money obviously compen~ sates for the loss of huge piles of niceness.

ambidextrous

Beverly Baker Fleitz

adj: able to use both hands with equal ease. A number of tennis players have used either hand in executing forehand and backhand strokes, only a few have been truly ambidextrous. The outstanding ex~ ample is Beverly Baker Fleitz, who switched her racquet from hand to hand, depending on which side the ball was coming to, with the result that she never hit a backhand! She was ranked No. 3 in the United States in 1954, and reached the final at Wimbledon in 1955.

Australian formation

n: the often upsetting tactic of a doubles team, in which the partner of the server stands at net on the same side of the court as the server. It is also known, somewhat perplexingly, as the American formation. In Davis Cup his~ tory, quite indepently and a number of years apart, each nation used it to defeat a doubles team from the other nation, so both countries have labeled the hateful ploy with the other country's tag. However, if you prefer not to foster nationalism, you can call it the tandem formation.

Backboard

n: a high wall, usually made of wood and painted green, with a white line painted on it the height of a tennis net, against which a person can practice strokes. The ball comes back at you much more quickly than if you were hitting it over a net into an opponent's court, so you have to be on your toes to practice effectively against a backboard, which makes it very good practice.

backcourt game

n: the court strategy of a player who prefers to stay near the baseline, and who seldom ventures to the net.

backhand

n: a shot hit on a player's left side by a right~hand player (or on the right side by a left~hander). In recent years a number of players have adopted two~handed back~ hand strokes, with both hands grasping the handle of the racquet in the fashion of a baseball grip, but the traditional backhand is still performed with one hand.

Don Budge

backhand grip

n: the way the racquet handle is gripped for backhand shots. If one tried to hit a backhand using the forehand, or Eastern, grip, the face of the racquet head would slant up at something like a 45~degree angle toward the sky. To prevent this, one slides his hand about a quarter~turn back onto the top surface of the grip, so that the face of the racquet head is kept perpendicular to the ground.

Those who use two hands on the backhand merely back up and strengthen the basic hand by adding the other above it onto the grip.

Ahh!

backscratch

n: the position of the racquet head, held over the shoulder and behind the back, between the shoulder blades, during the service motion. The term is used by tennis professionals in teaching a pupil how to serve. As the ball is tossed up for a serve, the racquet arm sweeps around high and to the rear, with the wrist cocked so that the head of the racquet drops down into the "backscratching position." It's the equivalent of a full wind~up in baseball.

bad bounce

n: an irregular rebound of the ball off the playing sur~ face. The complaint about getting a bad bounce might well have simply been listed in the section on alibis, but it is true that bad bounces often abound on any soft~ surface type of court, and even occasionally on hard~ surface ones. A shot that hits a line, particularly if the

(bad bounce cont'd)

line is tape, is prone to skid, and any surface irregularity is likely to occasion a bad bounce. The consolation is that bad bounces pretty well even out over the long haul, but that's scant consolation over the short haul if a bad bounce loses you a critical game.

bagel

Eddie Dibbs

n: slang for zero. This picturesque term was coined by Eddie Dibbs in describing a match in which he played, but it has been popularized by tennis writer and telecaster Bud Collins, who will report that the winning player of a 6~0 set has "bageled" the loser. (We pre~ sume that you don't have to be Jewish to know what a bagel is.)

balance

n: (1) bodily equilibrium or stability. Vital to keep on a tennis court as well as in your bank. Proper use of the arm that is not executing the stroke is the key ingredient to maintaining good bal~ ance. (2) the apparent equilibrium of the racquet. One of the aspects in choosing a racquet is whether it is head~heavy, handle~heavy, or evenly balanced.

Maria Bueno

ball

n: the round object that is hit back

and forth in a tennis game. Balls used to be white, and still are for the most part in England, the reason being partly tradition, and partly because they show up well on grass courts, of which England has a great many. But even tra~ ditional Wimbledon has finally succumbed to the yellow ball, which has virtually taken over all over the world on every surface, because of its greater visibility. There are orange balls, probably even more easily visible than yellow ones, and a combination orange~and~yellow ball, too, but they have never caught on. Balls are sold in pressurized containers of three in this country, and in boxes of four in England.

ballboys / ballgirls

n: the young people whose job is to retrieve balls that have to be cleared out of the way before the next service delivery, and see to it that the server has the ball(s) he wants before that delivery takes place. Ballboys and ballgirls are the caddies of tennis and, like many caddies in golf, often have gone on to become top play~ ers in their sport.

bandeau

n: a ribbon or scarf worn around the head. Various

(bandeau cont'd) types of headgear are worn by some tennis players, with an ordinary sweat~band around the brow being the most popular. A colorful bandeau, more like a hand~some scarf and held in place with a knot, has been affected

Pat Cash (wears one)

Yannick Noah (needs one)

upon occasion by such top players as John McEnroe and Australia's Pat Cash.

baseline

n: the lines that mark the two ends of a tennis court. A person who is serving must deliver his serve from be~hind the baseline. If he/she touches the baseline or steps over it into the court in serving, it is a fault. Receivers of a serve stand near their own baseline. During play, a shot that sails past a baseline is "long" and, obviously landing out of the court, is a losing point for the striker of it.

blooper

n: a lucky shot that wins a point as the result of a mishit. It usually results from striking the ball with the frame of the racquet, rather than the gut, or from a carry (or sling), which is today a legal shot. In these cases a completely unexpected and erratic flight luckily wins a point from a very annoyed opponent.

break

n: the loss of a game by the server. In better~grade tennis, having the serve is extremely important, and a set often goes along with first one player winning when he serves, and then the other player winning the next game when he serves. So when a server loses a game, it means that if his opponent merely holds his serve in the remaining games of the set, he will win it. In a tie~breaker, losing a point on one's serve is a minibreak, for the same sort of reasoning.

bubble

n: a huge dome~like construction, made of a vinyl~like material, that is used to convert outdoor courts into ones that can be used in the winter and in bad weather. Blown up and held up (like a bubble) by air pressure, and anchored to the ground, it can effec~ tively cover one or more courts, depending upon its size. It is essen~ tial to have a good air~ pressure machine that keeps the bubble standing, and a back~up machine as well in case the basic one conks out. Otherwise, like the walls of Jericho, the whole thing may come tumbling down.

bye

n: in a tournament, a free pass into the next round.

(bye cont'd)

It occurs when there aren't the requisite number of entries to fill out a draw sheet neatly and completely.

Cannonball

n: the fastest type of serv~ ice—hit flat and so severely that it booms into an opponent's box, ofen for an ace. The term seems to have first been coined by sportswriters with reference to Bill Tilden's tremendous serve. During the years in the 1920s when he dominated the tennis world, his serve was credited with travel~ ing 163.6 m.p.h. When facing a cannonball serve of that order, ducking would seem the better part of valor.

Bill Tilden

carry

n: the accidental hitting of a tennis ball in flight (almost invariably while at the net) so that it isn't struck cleanly. It is almost as if it were caught momen~ tarily in a net and then slung. The effect is that the ball stays on the strings of the racquet longer than it would with a clean hit, and usually flies off at so unexpected an angle as to be unreturnable. For years a carry, or sling as it is also known, was deemed an illegal shot and cost the striker of it the point. But since it isn't always

easy for an umpire or an opponent to detect with cer~
tainty, and often had to be called against oneself by the
player who committed it, it led to uncomfortable situa~
tions. Accordingly the shot has been ruled a legitimate
one in recent years, and a lucky point made off one,
even if inadvertent, is a winning point. The exception
to this ruling is explained under "double hit."

Centre Court

n: Wimbledon's most
hallowed ground, where
all its championship
final rounds have been
contested. Are you hop~
ing to be able to get a
good seat at Centre Court
for a late round in the next
Wimbledon tournament? Well,
as has been said about something
else, it is easier for a camel to
pass through a needle's eye.

Virginia
Wade,
star at
Centre Court
for the 100th
Wimbledon.

challenge round

n: the final round, between the defending champion
from the previous year and the person, or team, who has
won the right to challenge. Now obsolete, because today,
both in tournaments and in Davis Cup competition,
everybody starts from scratch. But once upon a time
and for many years, defending champions, or the de~
fending nation in Davis Cup competition, only had one
encounter, which was to try to beat off the survivor
who emerged from early~round contests to make the
challenge.

champion

n: the winner of a tournament. Regardless of whether it's an amateur local affair with a small plated cup as the prize, or one of the biggest professional affairs like an Open, where in addition to a stunning trophy there is a matter of several hundred thousand dollars that the title will earn the winner, a champion is still a champion. As Caesar said: "Rather be first in a little Iberian village than second in all Rome."

change a losing game

v: to adopt different tactics, in the hope of winning. Perhaps the best~known piece of advice in the literature of tennis instruction was Bill Tilden's "Never change a winning game: always change a losing game." He meant, for example, that if you have been winning by staying in the backcourt and trading drives, don't dream of getting fancy and storming the net so long as things continue to go well for you; but if you've been losing while sticking back there, then for heaven's sake start trying to play a completely different sort of game.

Evonne
Goolagong
Cawley

change of courts

n: the switching of play~ers from one end of the court to the other. This is ordained to take place at the completion of every odd game (the first, third, fifth, etc.), in order to balance out any advantages or disadvantages occasioned by wind, sun, background, or whatever.

chip

n: a short stroke that barely clears the net, usually executed with a chop. The chip is often used, particularly in doubles, to return the ball low and close to the feet of the server, who is rushing in from the baseline. The shot is sometimes called a dink.

choke

vi: to be unable to act efficiently because of nervousness or tension. "He choked" is the opprobrious description of a player who has seemed to have a match well in hand, and then suddenly goes to pieces and loses. Some players get a deservedly bad reputation because they choke frequently, but it must be admitted that there probably has never been a tennis player in history who hasn't experienced choking at one time or another.

chop

n: a short, sharp, downward stroke of the racquet that is intended to impart strong backspin to the ball. It resembles a slice, but the punch effect is more severe, and the angle of the descent of the racquet head is much closer to the vertical than is the angle described in a slice.

clay

Chris Evert

n: a form of earth, used to surface some tennis courts. Years ago almost all tennis players grew up on clay court surfaces because clay was available and practical to install. It is still the surface upon which most nations play the game and one of the four major tournaments, the French Open at Roland Garros stadium in Paris, is played on red clay. There have been many players who don't make much of a dent in major tournaments played on harder and faster surfaces, but who are almost unbeatable on clay.

closed stance

n: the traditional position of the body, sideways to the net, while making a shot. The player turns his side toward the net while in the act of hitting a shot, either from the forehand or the backhand side. This involves more than a twist of the torso: one leg should swing around and be so placed that the body doesn't face the net, but is sideways to it. In modern times, with so many hard-composition, lightning-fast surfaces, even great players can't follow traditional form all the time, and often hit from an open stance. Many have found they do better hitting from an open stance under any circumstances and do it all the time, but they are defying the teachings of the good book in so doing.

concentration

n: closely fixed attention to a matter. The importance of concentrating on every point is the first, fundamental lesson that tennis players are taught by professionals. It is as basic as learning the alphabet in school. There is a story that one unfortunate, being berated by his teacher between sets for his lack of concentrating upon his own and his opponent's play, replied that he had been so intense concentrating upon concentration that he forgot everything else.

Continental grip

n: an all~purpose grip of the racquet handle. It is halfway between the Eastern forehand grip and the backhand grip. It has an advantage over any other grip in that it can be used all the time and for any shot, and many superlative players adopted it exclusively for that reason. An outstanding example was Henri Cochet, one of France's Four Musketeers, who ended Tilden's and the United States' domination

Henri Cochet

of tennis in 1927. Most good players adopt the Continental for serving, since it helps impart spin, and for playing at the net, where play is so quick back and forth that it's obviously useful not to have to change one's grip. In fact, the only real disadvantage to using the Continental grip all the time is that one can't hit forehand and backhand drives with it with quite the force that one can with the Eastern and backhand grips, respectively.

control

n: consistency, steadiness of play. Many more points are won eventually because one player makes an error than are won by hitting a shot that's unreturnable. So a control player—one who makes less errors than his opponent even though the opponent makes more eye~catching brilliant shots—is a good bet to come out on top. This is particularly true at club~level tennis, but it's often been true at the highest levels of play as well.

cross~court

n: a shot that is hit along the diagonal from corner to corner, whether made from the forehand or the backhand side. In other words, not a straight shot down the center or along the sidelines. The cross~court shot is a basic one that is used constantly, and is a particularly important one for a receiver to execute in a doubles match, where every effort must be made to keep one's return away from the server's partner at net. A well~angled cross~court return is the usual best tactic.

Cyclops

n: the mythological Greek race of one~eyed giants. In recent years, in major tournaments, a new device has been installed that, by means of an electric eye, emits a sharp beep when a serve hits the surface of the court just past the receiver's box, thus relieving the linesman or the umpire of having to make a difficult call of whether or not the service was a fault. The irrepressible Bud Collins dubbed the electric eye "Cyclops."

Davis Cup

Arthur Ashe,
   former captain,
   U.S. Davis Cup team

n: the trophy, donated originally in 1900 by Dwight F. Davis for a dual match between the United States and England, now played for annually by countries all over the world. Matches are held throughout the year, with the final showdown taking place each December. Until 1927 only three nations had ever won it, the United States, Great Britain, and Australia, but the French took over for several years after that and today any of a considerable number of nations, some of them seeming quite unlikely, is apt to topple the former undisputed giants.

deuce

n: the score that is first reached in any game when each player has won three points—in other words, the score is 40~40. For some arcane reason, it is not correct to call 30~30 "deuce," even though the game situation at that stage is exactly the same as it is at deuce. And when we say that deuce is reached "first" at 40~40, it is because it well may not be the only time in the game. One player or the other must win two points in succession after deuce in order to win the game, and if that doesn't happen, and the next two points are split, the score goes back to deuce and the combatants try, try again. It's never been known to go on forever, but it can go on quite a number of times.

deuce court

n: the right~hand area of the court, as opposed to ad court.

dink

n: a slang term for chip.

Stefan Edberg

Anders Jarryd

doubles

n: play in which two players on one team oppose two players on the other. The doubles court is the same length as the sin~gles court, but it is 5 feet wider by virtue of the addi~tion of the two al~leys. Doubles involves team play and strategy, and calls for more tactical knowledge than singles, but it is not as strenuous. The result is that most young players prefer to stick to singles, but there invariably comes a time in every tennis player's life when he or she discovers the Joy of Doubles. Some specialists do so from the very begin~ning of their careers.

double fault

n: the failure to deliver the ball into the service box

in the two attempts that are permitted. If a server does not put his first service properly into play, a fault is called, but he is allowed a second serve on which to try again. (He may have even more, as explained under "let.") If he fails on his second service he has commit~ted a double fault and he has lost the point.

double hit

n: a return, similar to the carry, or sling, in being inadvertent and likely to produce an unintentional, crazy shot that confounds an opponent. Like the carry, it was illegal for years and lost the hitter the point, but like its relative it is now all right, for the same rea~son as given under "carry." The double hit does entail one exception, however, when it is still illegal and so loses the point. That is when the second hit is not inadvertent, but intentional, and that is an easy distinction for an umpire to see and to call.

draw

n: the list of competitors in a tourna~ment, indicating who will play against whom. A draw sheet is prepared not only to indi~cate the pairings for the first round of play, but who of those who emerge will play whom in later rounds, all the way to the finals, if they survive. If everything is to come out neatly, a normal field should have 8 or 16 or 32 or 64 or 128 players, but it's unusual to achieve that exactitude. That is why the bye was born.

Tim Mayotte

drive

n: a tennis stroke, hit from the back~court with substantial force. There are forehand drives and backhand drives.

drop shot

Ellsworth Vines, classic driver

n: a shot that barely clears the net and dies quickly as the result of backspin impart~ed to it. The drop shot is usually hit from a position close to the net, since, being the most deli~cate of shots, it's easier to ex~ecute safely from there. It can be hit either off a bounce or as a volley, the latter being a true skill shot. Drop shots should be made unexpectedly and must be executed well, otherwise they simply open the door for the other player to scurry and reach an easy, soft ball and murder it. If a drop shot isn't an outright, uncontested winner, it's likely to be a loser.

Eastern grip

n: the grip of the racquet handle commonly employed for forehand strokes. It's doubtful if any teacher has ever tried to explain the forehand grip any other way than to hold the racquet by its head, with the head held so that it's perpendicular to the ground and with the handle extended towards the pupil. "Shake hands with it," the coach will tell the pupil, and when he does he has mastered the Eastern grip.

Fault

n: a serve that is ruled not a valid one because (a) it does not land in the proper box, or (b) it is hit into the net, or (c) the server commits a footfault. Two faults in a row on the same point constitute a double fault, and they lose that point for the server.

Federation Cup

n: the trophy, competed for annually among teams repre~ senting many nations, that is the women's equivalent of the Davis Cup. Unlike that event, it is run off over a week's time at one site.

Hana Mandlikova helped Czechoslovakia win 3 consecutive Federation Cup titles.

fifteen

n: the term for the first point of a game won by a player. The origins of this unreasonable designation of a single point are unknown, and that's probably be~ cause it's so silly that nobody has ever wanted to claim credit for it. The same is true of thirty, as meaning two points, and forty as signifying three points. Why they are not simply called one, two, and three, respectively, pas~ seth all understanding.

final

n: the match for the championship of a tournament

(final cont'd)

between the two survivors from their respective halves of the draw.

firm wrist

n: what should be maintained for severe strokes, such as forehand and backhand drives. This is a hard thing for a squash player, turning to tennis, to remember, although there are some shots in tennis that are "wristy."

first in

n: a deplorable (and illegal) practice among certain casual (and neurotic) weekend players, which allows each server, on the first point of his first service game, to commit as many faults as he will, and the point doesn't get under way until he does deliver a ball properly into the service box.

Vitas Gerulaitis

flake

n: a rather crazy performer. A flake's antics are more likely to elicit amusement than indignation, as far as most bystanders are concerned. The prime example of a flake was Frank Kovacs. Bobby Riggs during his ballyhoo career as a senior player might be another. Some players like Ilie Nastase, Jimmy Connors, and John McEnroe have flaky characteristics, but they are less attractive than flakes.

flat serve

n: a serve that is simply smashed straight ahead,

without spin. When a server wants to power a serve as hard as he can, as in the case of trying for an ace with a cannonball, he resorts to a flat serve. It's rather like driving a stake high up into a wall with a mallet.

Flushing Meadow

n: the Long Island site of the Louis Armstrong Stadium, present home of the United States Open championships.

follow through

v: to extend past the moment of impact with one's arm and racquet head. No stroke should stop right after the ball is hit off the strings, even though the ball is then under way, for unless a player learns to follow through on his stroke, he will not be hitting effectively. It's essential on all strokes but it's particularly vital when serving, for it not only escalates power but also impels the server forward toward the net.

foot fault

n: a fault that is called because the server either touched the baseline with his foot while serving, or actually stepped over it and landed with a foot on the court before meeting the ball with his racquet. Jumping and being in midair while a service is being struck is legitimate, even if the server is over or past the line, but the ball must be hit before a foot lands.

footwork

Mikael
Pernfors

n: moving efficiently around the court.

(footwork cont'd)

Learning good footwork is as important as learning good technique in stroking. The combination of footwork and anticipation, both of which can be taught initially but can only become truly absorbed through practice and experience, is a foundation of playing sound tennis.

forcing shot

n: a shot made with such severity that it will win out~ right or else produce a weak return that the forcer can put away easily.

forehand

n: a shot hit on a player's right side by a right~handed player, and on the left side by a southpaw. It is almost in~ variably performed with one hand, although Pancho Segura and John Bromwich used two hands with startling success.

Pancho Segura

Forest Hills

n: the Long Island site of the West Side Tennis Club, historic former home of the United States championships, and the current home of the WCT Tournament of Champions.

forty

n: the term for having won three points in a game.

Game

n: a unit of play in which one player serves until a winner is determined, as follows: Four points won by a player wins him a game unless, before the fourth point is won, his opponent has tied him at three points each (deuce). Now one player or the other must win two points in a row before the game can be won. Otherwise the score reverts to deuce and the attempt to win two points in a row continues until it finally happens. That may be almost immediately, or it may take what seems like forever at the time. (In the 1987 French Open, for example, in a game between Ivan Lendl and Sweden's Joakim Nystrom, the score went back and forth from deuce to advantage to deuce for just under a half an hour before the issue was settled). Six games wins a set, except when it doesn't (see "set" and "tie breaker").

Grand Slam

n: the complete sweep in one calendar year of all four of the major championships: Wimbledon, the United States, the French, and the Australian. Only two men have ever achieved this, Don Budge in 1938 and Rod Laver, who did it twice, in 1962 and 1969. Among the women, Maureen Connolly turned the trick in 1953 and Margaret Court in 1970.

Rod Laver

grass

n: the prettiest and most pleasant surface upon which to play. But who ever gets much of a chance to do so except those who live in a climate like England's, where the regular light rains are ideal for maintaining grass courts—but only from mid-May to September at that? Most Americans have never seen a grass court except when watching

(grass cont'd)
Wimbledon on television.

grip

n: (1) the name for the part of the racquet that is grasped by the hand. A small grip is about 4⅛ inches around; a medium one, 4¼ to 4⅝; and a large grip is 4¾ or bigger. (2) with the addition of a defining word (backhand, Continental, Eastern, Western), the fashion with which one grasps the racquet.

gut

n: processed animal intestines, preferably from lambs; the finest (and most expensive) stringing for a tennis racquet. However, unless you're a ranking player and feel that you benefit from the small fractional edge in power that gut stringing may afford you, the chances are not only that you will be perfectly happy with nylon stringing, but won't know the difference.

Hacker

n: slang for an ordinary tennis player. The term was first used, with lunatic modesty, by Fred Stolle, referring to himself after he surprisingly won the United States championship in 1966 after not having been considered enough of a threat even to have been seeded in the draw. Bud Collins frequently uses the word on television when he's talking about a player who has no pretentions to being of exceptional calibre. Like you or me.

Fred Stolle

half~volley

n: a shot usually hit from midcourt, in which the ball is hit perforce at shoe~top level, immediately after it strikes the court. The ability to handle this shot effectively is a good guide in separating the sheep from the goats.

John McEnroe

hard courts

n: playing surfaces such as concrete, asphalt, macadam, and shale (thin layers of bedded rock arranged flat and fit~ ted like a mosaic).

Har~Tru

n: the artificial surface that must closely resem~ bles clay, as far as the playing conditions it affords. In many ways it's better than clay because it's eas~ ier to maintain, and dries out more quickly. When the United States championships, then held at the West Side Tennis Club in Forest Hills, decided to scrap its traditional grass courts in favor of installing a sur~ face that would accommodate all world players, many of whom had no grass court experience, Har~ Tru was the surface chosen. But when the tournament moved to Flushing Meadow short years later, it was decided that DecoTurf II would be the new surface of choice. The WCT Tournament of Champions, however, still takes place at Forest Hills, and is contested on Har~Tru.

heavy ball

n: a ball that seems to the receiver, when he meets it with his racquet, to have more than the usual weight. It is obviously not a matter of a ball's ac~ tual weight, but certain players seem to have a talent for combining speed and intense backspin to pro~ duce a heavy~ball effect upon the person trying to handle the shot, par~ ticularly at net, that is vaguely comparable to trying to stroke a shotput. Ken Rosewall's backhand was dreaded because it seemed so heavy a ball.

Ken Rosewall

high~percentage

adj: choosing shots that don't entail foolish risks and have a good chance of winning. High~percentage players get their first serves in play regularly. They put topspin on deep drives to keep the ball in court. They keep the ball away from the net when receiving in a doubles match, alternating deep cross~courts, dinks, and lobs over his head. When they do attempt a low~percentage shot, like trying to pass the net man down his alley, it's only because the game score situation seems right for it, and to vary play enough to "keep the net man honest."

hitting down the line

ROSE-WALL

part. phrase: driving the ball close to the sideline and parallel to it. This tactic is used most often when a player is drawn to a corner and decides this higher~risk shot has a better chance of winning the point than if he made the safer, cross~court return that his opponent could probably reach at net and put away.

hitting down the middle

part. phrase: driving the ball straight down the center, the safest of shots to make. In singles, this tactic can be helpful for a net~rusher, in that it reduces the area into which an opponent is most likely to hit a successful pass~ ing shot. However, its primary use in doubles, where it may precipitate confusion be~ tween your opponents as to which of them should take certain balls.

hitting in front

part. phrase: meeting the ball well in front of the body. Not only should one step into a shot, but the ball should be met with the racquet face somewhat in front of the body on forehands, and well in front of it on backhands.

I Formation

n: two players on a doubles team caught so that one is directly in front of the other. This is a facetious term, borrowed from football, that is used in tennis to describe a catastrophic situation that sometimes arises

44 (I formation cont'd)

inadvertently in a doubles match. Doubles partners should always be side by side, never lined up.

in

adv: landing within the court. A player should call "In!" (against himself) when his opponent's shot has landed so close to a line as to make the decision as to whether the ball was good or not a difficult one to determine. Of course, if the ball was clearly out, even if only the tiniest bit, he should call "Out!" but he should call "In!" and make the gesture indicating the fact (like patting the head of a large dog several times) not only when he's sure the ball was in, but also when he's uncertain about it. That is the tennis code.

Jamming the receiver

part. phrase: serving directly into the receiver's body. Most serves are directed toward one side or the other of the receiver's box in an attempt to pass him, or at least make him stretch far out for the ball. Occasionally, however, it is an unexpected tactic to serve right at him so that he has less chance to prepare to swing effectively.

Harold Solomon

junk

n: shots that have no velocity. Just as there have been ex~tremely successful baseball pitchers who threw nothing but junk (knuckle balls, slow curves, etc.), so there are successful tennis players who do the equivalent in tennis terms. They never—well hardly_ ever—hit the ball hard. Instead they float up slices, and dinks, and drop shots, and lobs, and moonballs until their opponents drop through weariness or sheer exasperation, for a good junk player is infuriatingly steady, nearly never making an unforced error, and also seems tireless.

Keep your eye on the ball

Steffi Graf

v. phrase: to watch the ball so intently that, in theory, you actually see the strings make contact with it. Well...maybe... but there are countless high-speed action photographs of great stars that would disprove that theory. However, as a concept, the idea is good. You should certainly concentrate intently upon the flight of the ball as it approaches you, and see it hit the court in front of you and follow its path right up to the hit. Whether or not you actually see contact, or look away a moment before (as one would usually do in catching a ball) is moot. If you are at net, the chances are more realistic that you do see the actual contact.

keep your knees bent

v. phrase: to maintain a flexible stance. One's knees should never be locked on any tennis shot, or even when one is not actually involved in a stroke. At the very least they should be slightly bent when waiting to receive, or standing at net. Bending the knees very considerably comes into play on any shot that has to be stroked near the ground. Such a shot cannot be made well from an erect stance. One must bend the knees almost to kneeling position and get one's body down to the ball.

kick

n: the high bounce that a ball takes as a result of a good twist serve.

Kooyong

n: the stadium in Melbourne at which the Australian Open was contested.

Ladder

n: a competitive system of rating players on a continuous basis. At tennis clubs or communities, where there are a number of players who regularly are available to play against each other, maintaining a ladder is an alternative, or sometimes an addition, to having a tournament. A board is kept up throughout the season on which all the play- ers' names are posted, each on a separate nameplate that can be shifted up or down into a different slot, as

the result of a lower listed player chal~
lenging a higher one and beating him.

lawn tennis

n: the actual name of the game of tennis.

let

n: a shot or a point that is not
scored and should be replayed. The most
common form of let is a serve that ticks
the net, or even hits the net cord, and
lands in the proper receiver's box. A
let point is also called occasionally
when something that is nobody's
fault interrupts or distracts play,
such as a stray dog running across
court, or an earthquake.

Fred Perry

linesman

n: the officials who determine if a shot has struck
safely within a line, or is out. They haven't gotten around
yet to calling a linesman a linesperson, but they cer~
tainly should because a great number of
them are women. Actually, regardless of
sex, it is one of the worst jobs in the
world. If you do it perfectly, no one no~
tices or thanks you for it. On the
other hand, you've a very good chance
of being subjected to vilification if you
make a call that one of the many bad ac~
tors on the tennis circuit these days
doesn't like. What's more, a consci~
entious linesperson glues his/her

eyes to one particular line, and can't ever really relax and enjoy watching the match.

Lingering Death

n: slang for tiebreaker.

lob

n: a tennis stroke that lofts the ball. A lob is usu~ ally an attempt to clear the reach of an opponent who is at net, and if the lob is too short or too low, it presents an easy put~away for one's rival. A sim~ ple, uncomplicated lob back to one's opponent's baseline can be either an offensive weapon, or a defensive ploy when you are hard~pressed and need to gain time to get back into position. The lob is used more often in doubles than in singles, and the most skillful and satisfying lob is a topspin one, which requires a particular deftness of touch, and which is definitely an offensive weapon.

Zena Garrison

loop

n: a feature that is part of the stroking technique of some players. The loop sometimes is incorporated into the backswing of a serving motion. It's also a name used for a basic shot that is stroked from a point very low down, with the racquet head coming up extremely sharply and the wrist turning over during the course of it. This produces a topspin shot.

love

n: a score of zero. When a player has not won any points, or games, or sets, the word "love" is used to indi~cate that fact. For example, one player may lead another fifteen—love in a game, or three—love in a set, or may have won a set six—love. It is claimed that the word derives from the French word for egg, "l'oeuf," which would seem to ally it with that other piece of sporting vernacular, "the old goose egg."

low~ percentage

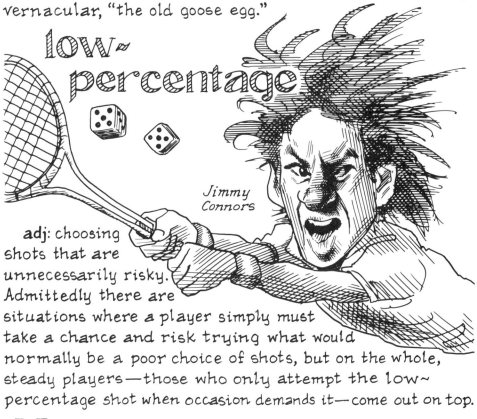

Jimmy Connors

adj: choosing shots that are unnecessarily risky. Admittedly there are situations where a player simply must take a chance and risk trying what would normally be a poor choice of shots, but on the whole, steady players—those who only attempt the low~percentage shot when occasion demands it—come out on top.

Match

n: a tennis contest. Most matches are best~two~out~of~

(match cont'd)

three affairs. That means that one has to win two sets to win the match, regardless of whether it's the first two in a row (in which case a third set is unnecessary), or the third set in case the first two sets are split. In the very biggest and most important men's tournaments, like the four Opens, matches call for greater stamina, since they are best~three~out~of~five contests, which may be decided in three sets but which may extend to the full five. Matches of more than four hours' duration are not at all uncommon, and some have gone more than six hours.

match point

n: that nervous moment when the player who's ahead can win the match by winning one more point. The one who is trailing gains a reprieve if he scores instead, thereby "saving a match point."

midsize racquet

n: a compromise~size racquet head. When the oversize was developed a few years ago, it clearly had advantages over the traditional racquet's smaller racquet head, but so many nondescript players

Pancho Gonzales

liked it that better players tended to be supercilious about it, and were reluctant to take it on. Then the midsize came into being, larger than the one but smaller than the other, and it has become the favorite of most of the tennis world.

minibreak

n: the loss of a point by the server at any time during the tiebreaker. It will cost him the set if his opponent then manages to win his remain~ing serves.

mixed doubles

n: a doubles game in which a male~female partnership opposes a similar pair. Under most conditions it's a pleasant form of tennis, but it is felt that a substantial portion of divorce lawyers' busi~ness stems from husbands and wives deciding to partner each other in their community's mixed doubles tournament.

Steffi Graf

Gabriela Sabatini

monkey~on~my~back

n: a jinx, involving a streak of defeats by a certain oppo~nent. The term is not exclusive~ly tennis's, but it belongs in the

(monkey~on~my~back cont'd)
lexicon of tennis perhaps more than
in any other sport. When players final~
ly defeat opponents who have consis~
tently been beating them over a long period of time,
they are likely to claim, "I finally got the monkey
off my back." (Maybe they did, and maybe they didn't.
The next few matches will tell).

moonball

n: a ball hit extremely high in the air, like a lob,
but not with the same offensive or defensive motives
that inspire, or force, a lob. A moonball is hit during
a baseline rally with the intention of upsetting an
opponent's pace and rhythm, to possibly precipitate
an error or a weak return shot. Moonballs are
often answered with return moonballs, that
being a rather safe
way of circumventing
danger, and when
that happens and per~
haps continues, the
whole affair seems to
degenerate, and the gal~
lery starts whistling.

Net cord

n: the white canvas
band along the top of the
net, which a low shot
sometimes ticks and then
sails over. During the play
of a point, this is usually

of no significance and play continues, but sometimes contact with a net cord produces so erratic a result that the ball is unreturnable. If a ball hits the net cord on a serve, and the serve lands in the proper box, a let is called and that attempted serve simply doesn't count at all and is retaken.

net game

n: the court strategy of a player who prefers to get up to net and stay there, instead of remaining in the backcourt. His instinct is to volley, so he tries to attain the best position from which to do so. It is the opposite of a backcourt, baseline game.

Lori McNeil

net judge

n: a tennis official who hasn't much to do. His job is to sit on a chair between the umpire's stand and the net post, keeping a finger or two on the top of the net cord on all serves, so as to judge officially whether a let ball should be called as the result of a service having nicked the cord, in which case he will feel the tremor on his finger. Since, when this happens, almost without exception everybody in the place realizes it happened, either because it's obvious visually, or the tick is heard, or both, the net judge is by-and-large an unnecessary official, and is more to be pitied than censured.

nicking the line

part. phrase: hitting a ball so that it comes as close as possible to landing outside the limits of a court, but actually, even if most of the ball has landed out, has had a tiny portion of it clip the line, which means the shot was good. It is the role of the linesman, peering along that line, to render decision, and it invariably subjects him/her to catcalls, whistles, and jeers from partisans in the stands, regardless of how far away they may be sitting, or at how poor an angle.

no ad

n: a scoring system in which the first player to score four points wins a game. It is not necessary to win by a two~point margin, so if and when 3–3 (the equivalent of deuce) is reached, the next point decides things. No~ad scoring shortens the playing time of a set.

no man's land

n: that portion of a court just about midway between the net and the baseline. The term, borrowed from military vernacular, depicts the area on a court where

one ought not to encamp, because it's a hazardous position. A person standing flat~footed there is too far forward to take a ball comfortably on the bounce, but not far enough forward to be able to volley one ef~fectively. He/she is often forced to play a half~volley, usually a defensive shot that is more likely to lead to a losing point than to a winning one.

ntrp

abbr: national tennis rating program, the simple but useful self~placement method of evaluating one's skill level. Its value is that strangers can find opponents more or less of their caliber. There are 13 categories ranging from 1.0, 1.5, 2.0, 2.5, etc., up to 7.0, and each specifies clearly just what you must be able to do consistently to justify being in each category. A player just starting the game is rated 1.0. A highly skilled tournament player who has achieved USTA national ranking is a 7.0. A 4.0 player isn't at all bad, and a 5.5 player is very good in~deed, and would be a con~tender at the highest~level club or park cham~pionship.

Carling Bassett

nylon

n: man~made filament used for rac~quet strings. It is not damaged by damp weather, and is cheaper

(nylon cont'd)
and more durable than the gut it largely has replaced
for all except the most
high~ranked and/or
well~heeled play~
ers.

Boris Becker

Open

n: a tournament in which
both amateurs and profession~
als can compete. For many years tennis tournaments
were divided strictly between amateurs on the one hand
and professionals on the other. All the major champion~
ships were for amateurs only, which meant that most
of the world's best players remained amateurs, since
the only professionals who made substantial money
were the one or two every few years who had made the
very top in amateur ranks, and so could attract crowds
to see them play. In 1968 tennis finally followed golf's
lead and made the major tournaments Opens. Prize
money (rather than just trophies) was put up, all the
good players did turn professional, and a new era of
tennis was born.

open court

n: that portion of a court left undefended. The player
has been drawn so far out by a previous shot made by

his opponent that he has no chance of getting to the next shot his opponent is almost sure to hit.

open stance

n: the posture of a player who hits the ball while facing the net. It's contrary to traditional teaching, but for a variety of reasons, including the fast pace of to~day's play, many players now favor an open stance.

out

adv: landing outside court limits. Always called with em~phasis in normal, unumpired play, since it carries a note of exultation along with it. It means that the player who has made the call, being the one who is close enough to be in a position to do so, has won the point. Linesmen in big tournaments are apt to be equally em~phatic in making this call, but that's because it's their big moment to be on stage.

overhead

n: a ball stroked at full arm's length high above your head. Al~though it may be exe~cuted from any spot on your side of the court, it is usually a finishing~off stroke taken at or near the net, when an opponent's lob hasn't been lofted well enough

Yannick Noah

*Pam
Shriver*

(overhead cont'd)
to clear your reach. Although an overhead is sometimes cleverly angled away, it is much more of~ ten smashed away like a first serve, which it resembles.

oversize racquet

n: a racquet with a substan~ tially larger head than pre~ vious racquet heads had ever been. The Prince Com~ pany introduced the over~ size a few years ago, and it caught on so well that every manufac~ turer copied it. Its advantage is that its larger head surface area is kinder to balls not stroked perfectly at the central point of the stringing. The oversize still has many adherents, but a somewhat smaller compromise head, the midsize, has pretty well taken over from it.

Passing shot

n: a shot, usually a drive, that is hit so hard and so accurately that an opponent, in what would seem to be a good position at the net, is unable to reach it. Invariably a passing shot is hit down the line. The slang term for having achieved one is "threading the needle."

penalty

"Nasty"

n: a punishment for a breach of conduct. In major tourna~ment matches, the umpire in charge is em~powered to im~pose a penalty if a situation seems to justify it. Offenses range from taking too much time between points to berating offi~cials past endurance, and include many infractions such as throwing one's racquet in disgust or making obscene gestures. Penalties range from a first warning, or loss of a point, to disqualification and even a stiff monetary fine.

poach

v: to move aggressively in doubles, involving tres~passing on ground not normally with~in the territory you're supposed to cover. The partner of the server, instead of holding his/her po~sition at the net, breaks to~wards the center, hoping to cut off and volley away the nor~mal cross~court return expect~ed from the receiver. This can turn out to be a mistake if the receiver spots the move in time to hit his return of serve down the line in back of the poacher.

point

n: the smallest unit of scoring, awarded at the end of each exchange to either the server or re~ceiver. Winning four points wins a game, unless it doesn't (see "game").

pro set

n: a quick match consisting of a single, longer set. Instead of playing the usual three sets, only one is played, but a greater number of games is required to be won—usually eight, but sometimes more. In any case, if and when the games are tied at one game less than the requirement to win, say at 7–7, the issue is decided by playing a tiebreaker.

professional

n: one who plays, or teaches, or does anything connected with the game, including en~dorsing products, for money. The word's antonym is "ama~teur," meaning a player who doesn't play for or accept mon~ey. Since nobody is likely to offer money to any but the best and well~publicized players, "professional" has also come to mean someone who is highly skilled, while "amateur" conveys the image of a tyro.

John Newcombe

public courts

n: tennis courts that are inexpensive and are open to all, as opposed to private courts, such as clubs. The beauty part of public courts is that one doesn't have to take out a mortgage on one's home in order to play tennis. The Catch~22 is that you're likely to have to wait an hour or two before getting onto a court, and when yo do, it may be quite primitive and in poor condition. However, there are exceptions, such as Jimmy Evert's wonderful Holiday Park, in Fort Lauderdale.

Ivan Lendl

Quarterfinals

n: that stage of a tournament when the completion of the early rounds has left only eight survivors. Since quarterfinalists are likely to have been the seeded players for the most part, four excellent matches are in store for the spectators, so attending this round is a good choice to make if you're limited as to the number of times you can attend.

questionable call

n: a bounce so close to the line that you cannot be sure whether the ball just caught it and was in, or failed to do so and was out. In a match that has no linesman or umpire, the player who makes the call always stands to lose the point if he calls the ball good, and to win the point if he calls it out. So any question~ able call should be called good, or the person making the call doesn't understand the tennis sportsmanship code. Saying "I'm not sure—let's play it again" is a lamentable ploy, used too often by people who should know better.

quick serve

n: a serve delivered before the receiver is ready. A receiver is entitled to walk to the spot he selects and to get into a ready position, once he sees where the server is standing, without having to worry about a serve being shot at him before he expects it. A serv~ er is not required to call "Ready?" before he serves, but he does the equivalent in other ways: by taking his time, looking at his opponent to be sure he actually is ready, and then, and then only, serving. Otherwise he is guilty of quick~serving and the receiver is entitled to let the ball go and to ask that the serve be taken again. (Of course, if he plays the ball re~ gardless, he has accepted the serve as valid).

Pat Cash

Racquet

n: the tool of the trade. Also spelled "racket," but not by those who prefer attaching a little elegance to the game's nomenclature. We don't want racquetball to steal a franchise on the spelling, and there is no such thing as racketball.

rally

n: the hitting of the ball back and forth, as in a warm~up. "Rally" should not be confused with "volley," even though greenhorns may say "Let's volley a few before playing."

ranking

n: the rating of players' abilities based upon their records. The best player is No. 1 and then the others follow in order. There are world rankings, national, sectional, by age divisions, men, women, junior boys and junior girls, clubs, public parks — you name it. The purposes of ranking range from being a basis for seeding in a tournament to the distribution of money in the Nabisco Grand Prix.

Martina Navratilova

Roland Garros

n: the tennis stadium on the outskirts of Paris. It is the site of one of the four major tournaments in the world, the French Open. It is the only one of the four that is played upon clay—red clay.

round robin

n: a form of tournament. Most tournaments are elimination affairs in which, as each round is completed, the field is reduced by half, with only the winners going on to the next round of play. A round robin is much more a social event in which, if possible (and if not, as close as possible), every player (or team, if it's a dou~bles event which it usually is) meets every other play~er (or team) in turn. Losers play on right through the affair and don't have to retire to the sidelines. Winners are those who amass the most winning games. A good round robin is a lot of fun, but it takes somebody who really knows how to run one properly to avoid chaos.

runner up

n: the loser in the final round of a tournament.

He/she gets a considerably smaller trophy than the champion in an amateur event, and a considerably smaller trophy and check in professional tennis. But the runner up <u>does</u> get something.

Second serve

n: the serve that is allowed if the server has committed a fault on the first serve. Poorer players, timid about double~faulting, try to play safe on a second serve and more or less pat the ball into the service box. This exposes them to a vi~ cious return. A good second serve is delivered with a slice — enough so that it can be hit solidly with pace, but still land safely in the rear portion of the service box.

Stefan Edberg

TAKE 2

Seeding

n: the distribution of the best contestants in a tour~ nament draw, so that they will not be matched against each other in the early rounds. Seeding is an attempt, not always successful, to see to it that the star play~ ers will be the quarterfinalists (if there are 8 seeds), the semifinalists (if there are 4), and the finalists (if only 2 are seeded). In any case, the No.1 and No.2 seeds are always placed in opposite halves of the draw, as are the No.3 and No.4.

semifinals

n: the next to last round of a tournament, when all but four contestants have been eliminated. Therefore the semifinals consist of two matches, with the winners then meeting in the finals for the championship.

serve, service

n: the stroke that puts the ball into play on each point. The serv~ er strikes the ball so that it flies diagonally into the receiver's box. If he fails to do so he has committed a fault. Opponents alternate being server or receiver after each game.

service box

n: the designated area into which the server must make his service strike, in order for it to be in play. Both sides of a tennis court are marked off with two boxes, each 21 feet by 13 feet 6 inches side by side and extending from the net back toward more than halfway to the baseline. A serve has to be hit so that it lands in the box diagonally away from the side from which the serve is being made, and the server alternates from side to side with each point, with the receiver alternating accordingly. In doubles, of course, each box has a receiver defending it, so only the server shifts from side to side between points.

set

n: a group of six games won before the opposition has won five or, if the score becomes tied at 5—all, what~ ever higher number of games is required in order for one contestant or the other to achieve a margin of two games. The foregoing is the traditional way the outcome of a set is determined, but in recent years tiebreakers and no~ad scoring have come into play. Most matches are best~two~out~of~three sets, but the four major men's Opens are best~three~out~of five.

set point

n: the situation when the player in the lead will win the set by taking the next point.

shorts

n: trunks worn by men, and by some women, as the preferred lower~body tennis costume. The British Davis Cup player Bunny Austin was the first recognized star to adopt shorts, and he caused a sen~ sation doing so in the mid~ 1930s, up to which time long flannel trousers were demand~ ed for men.

H.W. (BUNNY) AUSTIN

BROKE THE SHORTS BARRIER

sidelines

n: the lines that mark the vertical boundaries of a court. They are 78 feet long and 27 feet apart on a singles court. The doubles sidelines, each 4 feet 6 inches further out, add an additional 9 feet to a doubles court, making it 36 feet wide. The parallel singles and doubles sidelines, on each side of the tennis court, form the two alleys.

singles

n: the tennis contest where one player faces one other player, as opposed to doubles, where a pair opposes another pair. Singles have nothing to do with bars or dating services.

sky hook

n: a spectacular way of hitting an overhead smash, with one's side turned to the net and a vicious sweep being made, almost over one's head, with a rigid arm. The name is borrowed from Kareem Abdul~Jabbar's basketball hook shot; the tennis stroke was "patented" by Jimmy Connors.

Jimmy Connors

slice

n: a stroke that starts high and finishes low. It is more flowing and less vicious than a chop. It too imparts backspin to a ball, but more by tilt of the racquet head than by the severe downward stroke of the chop.

slice serve

n: a service on which (for a right~handed player) the racquet face sharply brushes the top, right~hand side of the ball during the hit forward. It is the rec~ ommended serve for a second serve, since it produces an erratic bounce. Also, since the spin tends to bring the ball down faster than if it were hit flat, the serve can be hit hard~ er with some safety.

Guillermo Vilas

southpaw

n: a left~handed player. Many of the world's best have been and are southpaws, includ~ ing Rod Laver, Jimmy Connors, John McEnroe, and Martina Navratilova. Playing against a left~hander can be a traumatic experi~ ence, with their spin shots curv~ ing and bouncing the opposite way of a right~ hander's, and your normal instinctive efforts to hit to their backhands turning out to be hitting to their forehands. It's all pretty sin~ister. (The Romans knew it was—the Latin word for "left" is "sinistra.")

spaghetti racquet

n: a racquet invented by Werner Fisher, a West German, and used successfully in 1977 by several players including Mike Fishbach in the U.S. Open, in which he defeated much~higher~ranked Billy Martin, and then Stan Smith, in successive matches. Strung laterally with loose, knotted, thick multistrands of gut, it was ruled illegal subsequently on the basis that every hit with it was an intentional double hit.

spin

n: an abnormal rotation or whirl imparted pur~posefully to a ball by means of such strokes as the slice, chop, topspin, twist, etc., to produce an irregular bounce.

v: to twirl a racquet prior to a match, calling which side of it faces up. Like flipping a coin. The winner has the choice of (1) serving or receiving or (2) the side of the court. The loser has the remaining choice.

sponsors

n: the commercial establishments that, as an advertising and promotional expenditure, offer large sums of money to be competed for in tournaments. Two particularly involved sponsors have given their name to year~long events: the Nabisco Grand Prix Masters, for men, and the Virginia Slims Tour, for women.

stringing

n: slender cords of gut or nylon, woven in lattice~work form to make the face of the racquet head, and pulled taut so as to construct an effective hitting surface with which to meet the ball.

Sudden Death

n: the original proposal by Jimmy Van Alen for settling a set quickly, once the score had reached 6–6. It was the one used in major tournaments for a year or two until the professionals voted to scrap it in favor of its variation, the tiebreaker, which keeps things going a little bit longer. In Sudden Death, each player in succession serves two points, three for the last server, and the one who reaches five points first wins. If the score reaches 4–4, the receiver on the ensuing ninth point can choose in which court he prefers to receive the serve (or in doubles, which partner will receive), and this somewhat counterbalances the advantage the server has. Whoever wins that ninth point has won Sudden Death, 5 points to 4, and has won the set, 7–6.

sweet spot

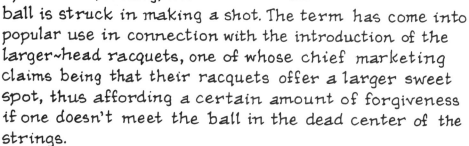

n: the small central area of the stringing upon which, ideally, the ball is struck in making a shot. The term has come into popular use in connection with the introduction of the larger~head racquets, one of whose chief marketing claims being that their racquets offer a larger sweet spot, thus affording a certain amount of forgiveness if one doesn't meet the ball in the dead center of the strings.

T-2000

n: the trade name of what is generally recognized as the first commercially suc~ cessful metal tennis racquet. Introduced in this country in the mid 1960s by Wil~ son, which took over the French patent held by Lacoste, it fell out of favor in the 1970s because its unique method of stringing produced what for many was an excessive trampo~ line effect. However, Jimmy Connors continued to use it faithfully and very effectively, and it's only been in the past year that he's deserted it and is experi~ menting with a prototype racquet of his own design.

Bjorn Borg

tactics

n: skillful maneuvering with respect to court position and choice of shots during the playing of a point. Planning the tactics one will use in a match is a part of strategy, which is more concerned with the long~range approach to a match, while tactics are concerned with immediate results.

tennis elbow

n: a form of bursitis. It is the most common complaint among tennis players, with innumerable theories on what causes it and just as many suggested remedies, none of which are likely to work. One extreme "cure" popular a few years ago was the wearing of a copper bracelet; the great Australian Tony Roche was one of many who resorted to it. However, even if it doesn't cure, an elas~ tic or leather brace can help ease pain until, with luck, Time and Nature do the trick.

tennis glove

n: a light covering for the racquet hand, used by some players to maintain a more secure grip.

tennis rituals

Jimmy Connors

n: a set form or system of rites. Certain rituals are part of *noblesse oblige* in tennis: the win~ ner rushing to the net to shake hands with the loser; bowing, or curtsying, to the Person~ ages in the Royal Box at Wimbledon, etc. But other rituals are purely personal, such as bouncing a ball *x* times in front of one be~ fore tossing it up for a serve.

(tennis rituals cont'd)

When X becomes more than 6 — and it does, it does, with some players — a case can be made for justifiable homicide.

tennis television

n: a communications medium, largely responsible for the incredible tennis boom that reached its peak in the 1970s. Two tele~vision broad~casts, each being seen by more than 50 million viewers, were particularly important in this respect: the unforget~table five~set duel between Rod Laver and Ken Rose~wall in the 1972 WCT championship final, and the 1973 challenge match between Bobby Riggs and Billie Jean King. On occasion, there has been more time allotted on the air to tennis on a single weekend day than was accorded the sport over a full year prior to 1968 and the introduction of Open tennis.

tennis whites

n: the traditional color and costume for tennis wear. Although tennis shirts, shorts, dresses, and ac~cessories now come in more colors than the rain~bow, and have been adopted by most players (some with more of an eye to fashion than to competition), there are many who still consider all~whites not only the right garb from an historic standpoint, but also the best looking. There are many sacred grounds where all~white is compulsory for players, so watch your step and your ward~robe if you're invited to Wimbledon or to Forest Hills, for example.

tennis whites,
a la
Anne
White

tension

n: (1) the degree of tautness used in the stringing of a racquet, expressed in pounds. A racquet strung at 80 or more is a very tightly strung racquet — Bjorn Borg preferred that. A racquet strung around 50 is a comparatively loosely strung job — John McEnroe favors that. (2) the extremely nervous condition that invariably descends upon both players when the score reaches set point, and then even more when it reaches match point. Possibly it reaches its peak the night before an important match, when there's time to think about it?

thirty

n: the term for having won two points of a game.

tie

n: (1) the score, temporarily, when the games in a set (or the sets in a match) are even. But neither ever ends in a tie; tennis is played out to a conclusion. (2) a Davis Cup meeting between two nations. The Davis Cup Tie is comprised of two singles matches on

(tie cont'd)

the first day, a doubles match the second day, and two other singles matches on the third day, so winning three matches assures a nation's victory. The two singles matches on the third day cannot pit the same players against each other who were opponents on the first day, but usually the same players simply are drawn against the players of the other nation whom they didn't meet on the first day.

tiebreaker

n: the most accepted modern method for settling a set quickly once the score has reached 6—6. A variation of Jimmy Van Alen's Sudden Death, this doesn't end matters quite so abruptly. The first person to serve does so from the right~hand court, for one point only. From then on, as the serve alternates back and forth, each player serves two points, starting on the left~ hand court. Seven points wins, but if the score reaches 6—6, a player, or team in doubles, must win by a two~point margin. That is why the tiebreaker's nickname is Lingering Death—it's possible for matters to go on for quite a while before the two~ point winning margin is attained. When it is, as in Sudden Death, the score of the set is posted as 7—6.

Margaret Court

time out

n: a respite from play that, in a major tournament at least, is strictly regulated. Players have 30 seconds after a point is completed in which to serve and put the ball into play again. A 90~second respite is granted when the players exchange sides of the court. A time out of 3 min~ utes can be granted when an injury occurs, but this is only allowed at the um~ pire's discretion.

Mats Wilander

topspin

n: that variation of spin produced by stroking a ball with a brushing motion that starts low and finishes high. The ball takes on an unusually speedy rotation in the direction in which it's traveling, which brings it down faster than ordi~ narily, and adds a considerable margin of safety to the shot. Two topspin players, pitted against each other, can sus~ tain a rally a long time. During the last French Open, when this happened, the telecaster Bud Collins said that tennis was getting a severe case of terminal topspin.

toss

n: the upward, light, and easy throw from the hand, used by the server to place the ball into position for the service hit.

tournament

n: a series of contests among a number of players, programmed in advance with respect to who plays whom, resulting in an eventual winner of a championship.

twist

n: another variation of spin, pretty well confined to the serve. It is the opposite of a slice serve, in that the ball is stroked from its left side across toward the right, in the course of hitting forward. (This is for a right~handed player.) This produces the opposite errat~ ic bounce from the slice serve, but it's a more difficult one for the server to execute, and it isn't a part of most play~ ers' reper~ toire.

Chris Evert

two~ handed shots

n: shots made with both hands gripping the handle of the racquet. Quite rare until recent years, the two~ handed backhand has gained great popularity as the result of its impressively successful use by players of the stature of Chris Evert and Jimmy Connors. Two~handed forehands are seen much less frequently, but they too have been employed for many years by stars, such as John Bromwich of Australia, and Pancho Segura.

Frank
Hammond

Umpire

n: the chief official of a tennis match. He runs it and announces the score after every point. In very im~ portant tournaments he is as~ sisted by linesmen, net judges, etc., but often the umpire is the sole arbiter.

underhand

adj: performed with the hand below the level of the elbow. Beginners may hit shots underhand, but it's com~ paratively rare that any good player does. A lob, particularly a topspin lob, or a half~volley pick~up shot could be excep~ tions, and certain topspin drives might fit the dictionary defini~ tion, although they are more sidearm. No player worthy of the name ever served under~ hand...with one remarkable exception. Betty Nuthall of Great Britain was one of the world's best women players from 1924 through 1927, during which time she always served underhand.

Manuel Orantes

underspin

n: that variation of spin pro~ duced by stroking a ball with a motion that starts high and finishes low. In other words, the opposite of topspin. Under~ spin is imparted to the ball on chops and slices, and it is par~ ticularly effective on a drop shot, making the ball die quickly off the bounce.

unforced error

n: an error that loses the point, committed by a player who was not being forced on the shot and should have been able to make a successful one. The mark of a great steady player is that he commits so few unforced errors. His opponent has to beat him: he refuses to beat himself.

upset

n: an unexpected result, when a favored player is beaten by a player who is ranked well below him or her. In a tournament, when a seeded player is beaten by an unseeded one, it's an upset.

USTA

abbr: the United States Tennis Association, ruling body of the game in this country. Until a few years ago it was USLTA (United States Lawn Tennis Asso~ ciation), but in a concession to realism, if not to tra~ dition, the name and the initials were changed.

VASSS

abbr: the Van Alen Simplified Scoring System. VASSS was Jimmy Van Alen's first attempt to streamline tennis scoring, and it used the same points~won scoring as in table tennis, but with 31 points needed to win. His intensive efforts to put it across met with some success with the pros for a while, but not enough to be adopted generally. Never a man to give up easily, Van Alen then invented Sudden Death, which led to its offspring, the tiebreaker, and so finally succeeded in sprucing up and shortening what might otherwise be dreary, marathon matches.

vibration

n: the rapid to~and~fro motion imparted to the strings of a racquet when the ball is hit, which transmits itself through the frame to the handle and the grip. Excess vibration, for one reason or the other, is often held accountable for the sizable number of tennis elbow complaints that exist.

Althea Gibson

volley

n: the act of returning a ball by hitting it in flight, before it can touch the court surface. A volley can be executed from any place on the court, but it's usually employed as a way of making one's way to net, and as the stroke made when at net.

(volley cont'd)

"Volleying" is sometimes loosely, but incorrectly, used to describe an extended exchange of shots, as in a warm~up period, but the correct term for that is "rallying."

Warm~up

n: any of a number of acts taken prior to playing, in an attempt to loosen up and condition the body. Part of a warm~up would be stretching exercises and jogging in place; an invariable part of it is rallying with one's opponent before starting a match.

WCT

abbr: World Championship Tennis. The professional group, founded by Lamar Hunt, which stages its indoor championship in Dallas, played every spring, and its out~door Tournament of Champions at Forest Hills. Both events have become very important fixtures in pro~fessional tennis.

weight of racquet

n: the weight of a tennis racquet frame, strung. Very often racquet weights are merely in~dicated with a marking along the handle: L (for light), M (for medium), and H (for heavy), with the range on the scales being something between 12 and 15 ounces — a medium would probably weigh in

Jack Kramer

at about 13½ ounces. There is a swing today toward
light racquets, probably because of the development
of graphite frames, which, although light, add the
force to a shot that heavier frames did, when
frames were made of wood.

Western grip

n: a well~recognized but somewhat
unusual grip. It has been used with great effective~
ness by players of note both in the past ("Little Bill"
Johnston and Bjorn Borg) and in the present (Jimmy
Arias and Kathy Jordan). If you lay a tennis rac~
quet down flat on the ground, and then pick it up by
the handle, you have taken the Western grip. It's
the opposite of the Continental grip, since your hand
is slightly under the handle rather than slightly on
top of it. The Western grip almost forces you to hit
every shot with topspin.

whiff

n: the actual missing of a ball with the racquet. This
practically never takes place except to a rank begin~
ner, but if an erratic bounce or a sudden gust of
wind causes you this embarrassment, you can always
say that you have a hole in your stringing.

Wightman Cup

n: the trophy competed for annually between a wom~
en's team from the United States and one from Great
Britain. The trophy is named after a legendary figure
in American women's tennis, Hazel Hotchkiss Wightman.

Wimbledon

n: the site of the British Open, and as sacred ground for tennis as Mecca is for Islam. Wimbledon retains just about all of its traditions over its more than 100 years of history, and is all the better and more honored for it. Grass courts and all~white tennis costumes are part of the tradition, but so are the best strawberries and cream in the world!

Wood

n: the substance beneath the bark in trees, fashioned by man to make many objects, including frames for tennis racquets. Wood frames have been supplanted to a large extent by metal, composite, and graphite frames, but you can still buy excellent (and considerably cheaper) wood frames, and there are players who continue to be faithful to them and love them.

Wrong foot

v: to hit behind your opponent. After pulling one's opponent off to a corner, one hits his return shot back to that same corner, instead of to the more obvious wide open court towards which he will naturally be running full tilt.

Xceed Xpectations

v: one of Hazel Hotchkiss Wightman's remarkable alphabet of alliterative maxims in her famous 1933 book, *Better Tennis*. Starting with Always Alert, she hurdled all the difficult letters successfully including Q (Quash Qualms), and finished the final three letters in high style, starting with this one. It is also hard to beat her final two letters, Y and Z, so this author won't try, but instead will include them with a nod of thanks to Mrs. Wightman and also to Herbert Warren Wind, whose brilliant article in *The New Yorker* about her brought all this to the author's attention.

Yell Yours!

v: part of Mrs. Wightman's philosophy in doubles of being a talk-it-upper with your partner in a doubles game. The well-intentioned shout " Yours" can often actually be helpful in resolving which player should take a questionable ball, according to Mrs. Wightman, but just as often it turns out to be either pa~ thetic or comic or both.

Zip Zip

exclam: the staccato delivery expounded and used by Mrs. Wightman to keep promising young players intent and up on their toes, with no thought that perhaps too much Zip Zip might eventually result in being Zapped.

Martina Navratilova

NICKNAMES

The nicknames of tennis players on the whole are less inspired than those bestowed upon professional athletes in team sports, like baseball and football. The rough camaraderie of locker room and playing field peers in such sports produces more picturesque nicknames, both affectionate and venomous, than the comparatively sober one~on~one relationships in tennis. The result is that on the whole an Ivan Lendl is simply Ivan, and a Martina Navratilova just Martina. But there have been, and are, exceptions:

Henry Wilfred (Bunny) Austin

Several things about Austin have been all but forgotten: (1) that he was the other stalwart on Great Britain's Davis Cup teams of 1933, 1934, 1935, and 1936, who, along with Fred Perry, won and held the cup against all comers, (2) that he was the first famous player to forsake long white flannel trousers for white shorts in a big tournament, causing much consternation, (3) that his name was Henry Wilfred, a fact that required much research to unearth, since he was never reported as anyone other than "H.W. Austin" (sometimes) or "Bunny" (practically always).

Boris (Boom~Boom) Becker

His tremendous service as he burst upon the major tennis scene, as a teen~ager, earned Becker his nickname at the time. He never cared much for it and let his feeling be known enough that few players would use it in his hearing today, even though the service is just as booming as it ever was, and maybe more so.

Jean (**The Bounding Basque**) Borotra

The most flamboyant of France's superb Four Musketeers, who ruled the tennis world from 1927 through 1932, Borotra was the epitome of dashing, energetic style, which, along with his having been born in Biarritz, earned him his nickname.

J. Donald (**Donald the Red**) Budge

It's doubtful if anyone actually called Don Budge "Donald the Red" in casual conversation, but that eminent chronicler of tennis history, Allison Danzig, who covered the game for 50 years for *The New York Times*, often referred to him that way during the years that Budge dominated the tennis world as solidly as Eric the Red once did Norway. In both cases, "the Red" obviously referred to a flaming thatch of red hair.

Maureen (**Little Mo**) Connolly

Maureen Connolly's unparalled success on the courts as a youngster, combined with her attractive manners, made her an idol and inspired her affectionate nickname. Her feats were incredible. She won the U.S. championship at the age of 16 in 1951, and over the next three years won nine major world championships—before she was twenty —including the Grand Slam in 1954! Had it not been for her tragic equestrian accident, her record might well have surpassed that of any other tennis player who ever lived.

James (**Jimbo**) Connors

"Jimbo" isn't that much of an extension of Jimmy, but Connors has always inspired perhaps the most vociferous of galleries who love his every antic, and their "Jimbo" is a term coined out of their admiration and enthusiasm. Even those who don't approve of Connors's showboating cannot completely resist his appeal as a colorful combatant.

Richard (**Pancho**) Gonzales

Anyone with Mexican forebears is apt to be nicknamed "Pancho" in the United States, so that's what happened to Gonzales (whose real name was Gonzalez but who got tired of telling people the right way to spell it and took the easy course out). Gonzales himself is as American as can be, having been born and brought up in Los Angeles.

Bryan M. (**Bitsy**) Grant, Jr.

The "Giant Killer" was 5 feet 4 inches tall and didn't quite weigh 120 pounds, but he was one of the greatest retrievers and control artists who ever played tennis. He took Don Budge and Fred Perry to the edge of exhaustion each time he played them, and holds victories over each, but his greatest triumph was beating Ellsworth Vines 6–3, 6–3, 6–3 in the National Championships at Forest Hills when Vines was ranked No. 1 in the world.

Harry (**The Fox**) Hopman

Hopman, an outstanding if not great player in his own day, became the shrewdest tennis brain in the world when he became the nonplaying captain of Australia's great Davis Cup teams. One time, after the Australians beat the United States, America's Tony Trabert confessed that his team had been beaten "by two babies and a fox." The babies were Ken Rosewall and Lew Hoad, both only 19 — the fox, of course, was Hopman.

William M. (**Little Bill**) Johnston

He was "Little Bill" to William T. Tilden's "Big Bill" throughout the years 1919 to 1926 when the two of them dominated the world of tennis. Although Johnston was inches shorter and many pounds lighter, he was Tilden's worthiest rival when Tilden was at his peak. Johnston defeated Tilden to win our National championship in 1919, but every year thereafter, although he often came close, he never was able to do it again.

René (**The Crocodile**) Lacoste

Youngsters may associate the name Lacoste, and the crocodile, only with posh sports shirts, but the name and the insignia have valid, historic tennis origins. Earning his nick- name for the unrelenting way he slashed up oppo- nents' games, Lacoste adopted the insignia when he founded his sports-gear company.

Rodney G. (**The Rocket**) Laver

Rod Laver's tireless, darting, powerfully soaring type of play inspired his nickname, for it carried him to unprecedented heights. His is one of the very few names that will elicit passionate arguments from many who claim he was the best tennis player who ever lived, with all due respect (as always) to Bill Tilden.

John (**The Brat**) McEnroe

"The Brat" is hardly a nickname anyone would use if addressing McEnroe in person, but it's a term that tennis journalists have employed in describing his antics ever since he first appeared on the scene. Anyone who has followed his career doesn't need to have the name explained.

Miroslav (El Gato) Mecir

No modern player is more quick and adept at pouncing upon any weak~ ness in an opponent's game, and ex~ ploiting it in unexpected ways, than Mecir. He is a Czechoslovakian so it's surprising that his nickname is the Spanish term for "The Cat."

Ilie (Nasty) Nastase

Since Nastase was the first of the obvious Bad Boys of modern tennis, the nickname he quickly earned seemed to fit his actions. He never appeared to resent being called Nasty, probably not only because it was a natural short version of his surname, but also be~ cause he rather revelled in his Bad Boy reputation.

Kenneth R. (Muscles) Rosewall

Rosewall's small but extremely powerful frame kept him a world contender for over three decades. His im~ pressive record (winner of the U.S., French, and Austra~ lian titles, and twice a finalist at Wimbledon) is matched by the way he accomplished it. In an era of the Big Game, he was essentially a baseliner who won with superb groundstrokes and by outmaneuvering opponents.

Francisco (Pancho) Segura

Sometimes dubbed "the Little Pancho," because Gon~ zales was the big one, Segura was born in poverty in Ec~ uador. He learned to play in secret and got such a local reputation that he was given a scholarship to the Uni~ versity of Miami, and he became the only man ever to win the U.S. Intercollegiate championship three years in a row (1942–1944). Although ranked No. 3 nationally twice, it wasn't until he turned pro in 1947 that he truly hit his stride and became one of the best players in the game. His two~handed forehand is almost surely the best ever seen.

Ion (**The Count, Dracula, Svengali**) Tiriac

Sporting more nicknames than anyone else in tennis, partly because he's recognized as a rather sinister mastermind and partly because of his facial appearance, Tiriac has successfully guided the careers of champions from Ilie Nastase to Boris Becker.

Wendy (**Rabbit**) Turnbull

The spunky Wendy Turnbull can cover court inde~ fatigably all day, and invariably seems to do so, return~ ing everything, even when she's up against a player who may at first sight seem to outclass her.

Helen (**Little Miss Poker Face**) Wills

America's premier sportswriter at the time, Grantland Rice, dubbed the young Helen Wills "Little Miss Poker Face," and the phrase caught on and stuck. She went about her business on a tennis court without displaying any signs of emotional turbulence, either in the face of triumph or disaster—just like Chris Evert later on. Kipling would have approved of both.

Slobodan (**Bobo**) Zivojinovic

Surely the fact that this powerful Yugoslavian play~ er has had a nickname bestowed upon him is more to be grateful for than any others in this book. Particular~ ly if you are a television reporter covering one of his matches.

BILL TILDEN

William Tatem Tilden 2d wasn't really tremendously big by today's standards of height, being not quite 6 feet 2 inches tall, but back in 1913 and 1914, when he first became a serious tennis player after leaving the University of Pennsylvania, he towered over most of the other young men of the era. Actually the nickname of Big Bill got attached to him some time later when he and Little Bill Johnston, who was less than 5 feet 6 inches and didn't weigh any more than 120 pounds, were matched against each other year after year in the championship finals, and teamed together to win the Davis Cup for the United States in 1920 and defend it successfully every year thereafter through 1926. So the names Big Bill and Little Bill were seized upon by every tennis writer in the country, and in other countries as well.

The fact of the matter is that despite his height, Tilden was something of a late bloomer as far as tennis was concerned. In 1913 and 1914 he was only a so-so player, his distinction being that he paired with Mary K. Browne both years to win the national mixed doubles title. However that was largely Browne's doing: she was unbeatable then and pulled off "the hat trick" both years, winning the women's singles and sharing in the women's doubles titles as well. But by 1918 Tilden had become a highly ranked player, first in men's doubles where he and his protégé, the young Vincent Richards, became one of the best doubles combinations that tennis has ever seen. Then, in 1919, Tilden's singles game had progressed so far that he reached the final at Forest Hills, and the first of the many "Big Bill" vs. "Little Bill" encounters took place. Billy Johnston, always a marvelous player himself and a great favorite of the crowd, was too good for Tilden that day, and won the U.S. title in three straight sets,

Taylor Jones

but it turned out to be the one and only time that Johnston ever bested Tilden in a major match.

For Tilden, ever the most brilliant of tennis strategists, realized that his regular backhand, which was somewhere between a slice and a chop, hadn't stood up to the relentless attack directed against it by Johnston's vicious Western forehand, one of the most lethal weapons in tennis history. Tilden spent the next year in Providence, Rhode Island, where he could play daily through the winter on Arnold Jones's private clay court, and he hit thousands of backhands until he developed an offensive weapon on that side that was the equal of his always powerful forehand. By 1920 he was ready to take on Johnston again and beat him, triumphing both at Wimbledon and at Forest Hills, and everywhere else. And so it continued to go from that time on for the next half dozen years. No one could stand up to him: until 1926 he never lost a championship match anywhere in the world, in an era in which there were tremendous competitive talents, all at their peaks. He not only beat all his countrymen such as Billy Johnston, Vincent Richards, and R. Norris Williams, but also the best the rest of the world could throw up against him, Gerald Patterson of Australia, René Lacoste, Jean Borotra, and Henri Cochet of France, and everyone else from England and South Africa to Japan.

Midway in 1922 it seemed that Tilden's brilliant career was going to be terminated. He cut the middle finger of his right hand on a wire fence and it became so badly infected that most of the finger had to be amputated, leaving only a small stump. After it healed it turned out not to matter at all. He won the U.S. championship, as usual, that September, and his best tennis years still lay ahead.

Tilden's racquet wasn't all that talked for him. He bore himself like the king of the courts he was, and he had a fine flair for the dramatic. When he entered a room, or walked out on the center court of a stadium before a match, his presence was so striking and dominant that he almost seemed royal. It must have cowed many an opponent before the first ball was struck, and he did intimidate USLTA officials and linesman, but never to frighten them into changing a call or making a decision in his favor. He simply had an imperious attitude towards anyone who struck him as not doing his job. He could not

tolerate anybody who was at all inattentive. He simply wanted things to **95**
be done correctly: he never berated a linesman for what he thought
was a bad call against him. Tilden was the epitome of fair play and he
never accepted a point that he thought he had won unfairly. He
became famous for the several occasions in important matches where
he thought a ball had been called incorrectly in his favor. He would
glare at the linesman or umpire, and then calmly proceed to toss the
next point to his opponent by purposefully hitting the ball out or into
the net. Tilden never wanted a point he hadn't earned.

In 1926 the brilliant French players, who had plotted Tilden's eventual downfall during years of having been beaten by him, finally
caught up and Lacoste won our championship that year and the next,
while Cochet took it in 1928, and the French also took over posses-
sion of the Davis Cup. But in 1929, at the age of thirty-seven, Tilden
won his seventh U.S. championship title, and the following year he
amazed everyone by winning Wimbledon for the third time. Then, in
1931, he was responsible for the biggest forward stride the new
branch of tennis had every enjoyed. He turned professional, and that
pioneered the way that led to what the game is today. Even after such
great stars as Vines and Budge and Perry followed, and even though
by then they could usually beat Old Bill, more people were prone to
turn out to see Tilden when he made an appearance than any other
player.

Tilden still continued to be a very fine player despite encroaching
age. When he was nearly fifty he defeated Ellsworth Vines, twenty
years his junior, in an important professional match in London. Tennis
experts and analysts have written that Tilden was still the best player in
the world when he was fifty-nine—but for one set only! He proved that
somewhat by winning first sets that year from three top-ranking
professionals of the time: Wayne Sabin, Frank Kovacs, and Bobby
Riggs.

But the Tilden story had a tragic end. With all his talents, and he
had many apart from tennis, having acted in several stage produc-
tions, written a number of stories and a novel, and played tournament-
class bridge, Tilden had a weakness. He never seems to have been
involved heterosexually with a woman nor, for that matter, homosex-

ually with a man, but there were always rumors that he dallied with young boys. They were never boys anyone knew, like his protégés in tennis, but seemed to be quiet pick-ups of unknowns, who Tilden felt would probably never come to the surface and never be heard of again. However, in his late fifties, Tilden picked up a boy in his car and was caught by police "in the act."

It was an astounding scandal, and Tilden was sentenced to serve a year on a prison farm. When he came out, although he continued to play some professional tennis, his reputation was shattered and he was snubbed by almost everyone. He couldn't find a job teaching, he was shunned in places where he used to be hailed, he became destitute and, one day, was found dead at the age of sixty in his tiny rented room.

In *Julius Caesar* Cassius, talking of Caesar to Brutus, says: "Why, man, he doth bestride the narrow world like a Colossus." Tilden is the one tennis player of whom that could surely be said as far as the tennis world is concerned, but although there is a noble statue of Fred Perry near the entrance of Wimbledon, there is no monument to Tilden of any sort anywhere, except a small headstone on his grave in the family plot in Philadelphia that simply reads:

William T. Tilden 2d
1893–1953

SUZANNE LENGLEN & HELEN WILLS

Unlike the rivalry of the two great women tennis players of modern times, Chris Evert and Martina Navratilova, who have faced each other across the net almost a hundred times, the two tennis goddesses of an earlier era, Suzanne Lenglen and Helen Wills, only met once on a tennis court. But what a meeting that was! It forever linked their names together and is thought of first whenever one or the other's name is recalled. Actually that shouldn't be the case, for their one encounter was not the true measure of either one's greatness, as will be explained, but it was *the* sporting event in a particularly dramatic sporting year, 1926, when Gene Tunney beat Jack Dempsey, the French Four Musketeers of tennis ended Bill Tilden's and the United States' long reign as winners of the Davis Cup, Rogers Hornsby's St. Louis Cardinals nosed out the generally acknowledged "best team ever in baseball," the New York Yankees, in the World Series, and Gertrude Ederle swam across the English Channel!

Of all of these events, the two biggest ones involved women, an amazing fact in view of how minor women's athletics were regarded back then. The Lenglen-Wills tennis match aroused such world-wide interest that it undoubtedly escalated the excitement engendered by, and adulation heaped upon, another female athlete, Ederle, when she performed her feat later that year. But the Lenglen-Wills match was made so memorable by the circumstances that surrounded it from beginning to end.

In February 1926, Mlle. Lenglen of France was possibly a shade past her peak. Her six triumphs in the Wimbledon championships had left her, at the age of twenty-seven, with no more worlds to conquer.

She had *never* been beaten in a match over a seven-year stretch,
except for one default to Molla Mallory in the 1921 U.S. event when,
after losing the first set, she declined to go on, saying that she was ill;
and she made a pretty convincing case for that contention when she
next met Mrs. Mallory, beating her 6–2, 6–0 in 1922, and 6–0, 6–0
in 1923. There was no one to challenge her except—possibly, but not
likely—a California girl named Helen Wills who, now just twenty years
old, had won the United States title three years running (although not
against the opposition or Mlle. Lenglen, who, after the 1921 experience, had not made the trip to Forest Hills again). Helen Wills was the
obverse of Suzanne: where Lenglen was possibly a shade past her
prime, Helen possibly was a shade short of reaching hers. After all, the
first of the eight Wimbledon titles she was to win later still lay more
than a year ahead.

Nothing epic had been planned. Miss Wills merely wanted to see
the French Riviera for the first time, and play a little tennis there. She
sent in her entry for a small tournament that was to be held at the
Carlton Tennis Club of Cannes, and without any apparent planning for
a dramatic confrontation, so did Mlle. Lenglen. That was the simple
background that set the place where the greatest match of tennis
between two women had ever been staged up to that point, and what
a strange and inappropriate place it was!

Located in a small space between four mean back streets in
Cannes, with the Carlton Hotel on one side and the back doors of a
garage, a scrawny hedge, and a saw mill flanking the others, the club
consisted of six courts—so squeezed in that three of them were
placed wrongly into the sun—and a little hut of one room that served
as a "clubhouse." It had one shower and a few washbasins, but no hot
water, no towels, no electric light. And the wooden stands alongside
the central court couldn't accommodate more than a couple of
thousand spectators at the outside. Even to attain that sort of attendance, workmen were busy bringing in wood and hammering extra
sections the very morning of the historic match, which was scheduled
for eleven-fifteen. Mobs of people crowded the ramshackle street that
ran alongside the court, trying to get in and quite willing to pay the
three hundred francs that a precious ticket cost. That was about

eleven dollars for an American, and since the price of a ticket to Wimbledon or Forest Hills in those days was only two or three dollars, the frantic effort from so many people to dole out three hundred francs was incredible. To a Frenchman, three hundred francs meant the equivalent of sixty dollars, which was absolutely beyond reason for many, who hustled to sit on the roof of the garage, prop ladders against a fence and stand on them, climb to the top of motor buses that were ranged behind the court, or scale the eucalyptus trees that lay just beyond the scrawny hedge. This match could have filled arenas like Wimbledon or Forest Hills without any trouble: it might well have filled a much vaster one like the Yankee Stadium had such been available, but it was held at the Carlton Tennis Club, and as a result, that rather miserable little club won a prominent place in tennis history.

Lenglen was a substantial favorite to win. She had never lost a match on her home turf along the Riviera or, for that matter, anywhere in France, and the first set held no surprises except for a momentary one when Wills won the second game. But Lenglen moved ahead and took control after the fifth game, and then ran the set out at 6–3. Still, Wills had put up a stubborn fight and started to do even better as the second set got under way. She actually took an early lead, and Suzanne stopped between games to partake of her restorative, which was not Gatorade but a sip or two of brandy. The set continued on even terms until the score reached 5–5, when a demonstration on the part of Lenglen's French fans had to be quelled by an admonition from Suzanne herself. However, tired and shaken as she obviously was by then, Lenglen finally reached match point, and when Helen smashed a shot deep to her forehand corner, Suzanne thought the ball was just out and the match was over, and rushed to the net to shake hands with Helen. But the ball was not out, the linesman insisted to the umpire, who had already begun descending from his chair. The players resumed position, the spectators went back to their seats or perches, the game went on, and Helen Wills won it to even the score at 6–6.

It was a courageous performance that Lenglen put on during the next five minutes, after she thought she had turned back her young

challenger only to find that the issue had not been settled. She won
two bitterly contested games to take the set 8–6 and the match along
with it, and then she came very close to collapse. It has been generally
agreed by all who saw the affair that, if Helen Wills had won that
second set, she surely would have taken a third and deciding set.

But that wasn't proven then, nor was it ever. Although a return
match was in the offing later that year in the French championships,
Miss Wills had an attack of appendicitis before then and was not able
to play in any of the great championships that year. And Mlle. Lenglen
turned professional late in the year, which in those days made any
rematch impossible.

A majority of players who actually faced Lenglen and Wills on the
court give the edge to Suzanne, saying she was incomparable, and
that no woman could ever beat her. However, Helen was certainly
stronger, hit the ball a lot harder, and had no peer during her reign,
just as Suzanne had none during hers. In any case, no woman player
could even be mentioned in the same breath as these two, whenever
people talked about who was the greatest of all time, until a quarter of
a century went by, and Maureen Connolly appeared, all too briefly,
upon the scene. Then it was another quarter of a century along the
line before we saw Chris Evert and Martina Navratilova. But each of
those, as they say, is another story, and their stories appear in other
articles in this book.

BILLIE JEAN KING

The achievements that Billie Jean King pulled off on the world's tennis courts are almost unmatched—in fact in one tremendously important area they are unmatched. Mrs. King won twenty Wimbledon titles during her career, which is one more than the previous record-holder, Elizabeth Ryan, ever did, and among Mrs. King's twenty she carried off the women's singles title half a dozen times, whereas all of Mrs. Ryan's victories were in doubles. Billie Jean also took the women's singles crown in the U.S. championships on four occasions and, in the decade from 1966 through 1975, virtually dominated the women's game. Her only rival who had some sort of parity with her was the great Australian player Margaret Smith, later Margaret Smith Court, one of the only two women ever to have achieved the Grand Slam (Maureen Connolly being the other).

Both of Billie Jean's parents were athletes, and her brother, Randy, pitched in the Big Leagues, so it wasn't surprising that little Billie Jean Moffitt took to all sports, particularly tennis, despite being a little overweight and very nearsighted. From her earliest days as a young teenager, she played a furious, aggressive, net-rushing game that contrasted sharply with that of the general run of steady, backcourt girl players of her generation. She wasn't the best in her class at that time, but in the next few years she far outstripped her American contemporaries and became a world-class player, whose all-out offensive tactics and devastating net game were feared by all. In 1962, still not nineteen years old and still Billie Jean Moffitt, she did the incredible and eliminated Margaret Smith, the favorite to win at Wimbledon, in the very first round! That triumph was short-lived and she herself was eliminated soon afterward, but the following year Billie Jean went all the way to the final where Margaret Smith took her revenge and, in doing so, won her first Wimbledon title. The rivalry

103

continued hot and heavy over the next decade, with the newly married Billie Jean King truly coming into her own in 1966, when she won the first of three successive Wimbledon titles, repeating in 1967 (in which year she also won her first U.S. championship), and then again in 1968. Billie Jean took Wimbledon again in 1972, 1973 and 1975, and after the 1967 win, captured the U.S. title another three times, in 1971, 1972 and 1974. When Billie Jean wasn't winning one or the other of the two great tournaments, Margaret Smith, who also played under her married name, Margaret Smith Court, in her later triumphs, took most of the others. True, there were years when Maria Bueno and Ann Hayden Jones and Evonne Goolagong and Virginia Wade upset one apple cart or the other, but that decade in the main belonged solidly to Margaret Smith Court and Billie Jean King. So in 1973, when Bobby Riggs came up with his celebrated challenge for a "Battle of the Sexes," it was logical that his proposition be made to one or the other or—as finally happened—to one after another. (The details of the two Battles of the Sexes are in the article about Bobby Riggs, which follows.)

Yet despite Billie Jean's wonderful record of achievement on the tennis courts, and the fantastic fanfare that accompanied the extravaganza of the Riggs match, what is most likely to be remembered about Mrs. King is the character and energy and honesty and foresight of the woman herself. She has always been one to blurt out whatever was on her mind without any equivocation, and she even won friends when she refused to be blackmailed by her female assistant who, attempting to obtain their house as a settlement factor when they broke up their relationship, first threatened to reveal that they had had an affair, and then did so. Billie Jean simply didn't deny anything but told the woman to get lost, and she won her case in court. It was typical of Billie Jean not to duck anything, even if it was unpleasant.

Ever the most colorful and controversial of tennis players, she uses outspoken and uninhibited language both on and off the courts to speak her mind, and through the years she has had plenty on her mind, largely to do with improving tennis and also improving women's place in the game. Years ago she was the most articulate spokesperson in insisting that tennis had to be taken away from the sepulchral atmosphere of the country club and channeled into places like the public parks and arenas for professional sports, or it could never achieve the popularity such a good sport deserved. She liked the idea of fans shouting in excitement during play, cheering for their favorites, even booing when they didn't like something or other. All this was sacrilege then, of course, but it has all come to pass, at least in some measure. Flushing Meadow is infinitely more of a circus atmosphere than Forest Hills ever was, and even Wimbledon is much less staid than it used to be. Tennis no longer is the exclusive province of the elite, but belongs to the masses, with gratifying financial rewards for everyone as a result. The rewards to the women players have escalated even more than to any other sector of the game, and Billie Jean has been largely responsible for it. Chris Evert, who took over domination of the women's game in the early 1970's, is quoted as having said: "She put money in my pocket and the pockets of all women tennis players. If it were not for her, we might still be playing an amateurish sport. She paved the way."

King was a leader years ago in trying to fight the stultifying domination of the women's game by the old USLTA, and was a chief protagonist in the formation of the Virginia Slims tour in the early seventies. She founded the Womens Tennis Association in 1973 and launched the Women's Sports Foundation the following year, and in 1987 she was inducted into the International Tennis Hall of Fame. She covers Wimbledon as an HBO color commentator and today, a dozen years past her playing prime, she's as active in tennis matters as she ever was. In fact, *World Tennis* magazine conducted a poll recently, asking their readers to vote who was the most important figure in tennis during the past thirty-five years. Billie Jean was chosen by forty percent of the respondents, more than double the votes received by the runner-up.

Taylor Jones

BOBBY RIGGS

Others may have had even longer tennis careers than Bobby Riggs, but there's little doubt that there has never been a world's champion player who has continued to capture the limelight of public attention, one way or the other, as long as has Bobby. Ever an exhibitionist and a chance-taker off the tennis court, Riggs was the most cool, calm, and solid performer of players, and as a result his reputation has never been quite as high as his playing genius merited. That magnificent player and champion Jack Kramer, who ascended Riggs' throne after Bobby left the amateur ranks to turn professional, wrote of him: "The greatest weakness of great players comes in overplaying the ball, i.e., hitting it harder than they should do or, in general, simply trying too tough a shot. *Only Bobby Riggs never overplayed his shots.*"

Riggs was three years younger than Don Budge, and although he was ranked among the world's best in 1937–38, when he wasn't quite twenty years old and Budge was the world champion, he took over in 1939 when he won the Wimbledon singles, men's doubles (with Elwood Cooke), and the mixed doubles (with Alice Marble), and then went on to win the U.S. National championship as well, and was ranked No. 1 at the end of the year. There is a story—it has become a legend in tennis history—that Riggs made a parlay bet before Wimbledon that year with a London bookmaker, putting up £100 at 3–1 odds that he would win the singles, 6–1 that he would win the doubles, and 12–1 the mixed event. Of course, had he lost any of the three events he would have lost the entire bet, but in winning them all the payoff was £21,600 (3 × 6 × 12 × £100), or $108,000 at the time. Whether the story is fact or not, it does sound like Riggs.

After winning the U.S. title again in 1941, Bobby turned profes-sional and truly dominated the pro circuit for half a dozen years,

107

invariably downing his old nemesis, Budge, in the process. Meantime Jack Kramer, three years younger than Riggs, had become the standout player among the amateurs, and when he turned professional in 1947, after winning both the Wimbledon and the U. S. titles and having been the mainstay of the champion United States Davis Cup team, the stage was set for a highly anticipated clash between Riggs and Kramer.

Their first meeting was scheduled for Madison Square Garden in New York City on the day after Christmas, December 26, 1947, and it not only snowed—it snowed so much and so long that the record of the Great Blizzard of 1888 was surpassed by mid-afternoon, and it was still snowing. A better than 20-inch blanket of snow had paralyzed the city. No transit lines or cars were moving. Thousands of people were stranded wherever they happened to be. There seemed no chance that any crowd to speak of could possibly make it to this great attraction that pitted the two finest tennis players in the world against each other. It seemed obvious they would have to play the match in comparative privacy.

A few minutes after 9:30 that night, with the snow now piled up to a depth of 26 inches outside, Kramer and Riggs hit the first balls of their match while 15,114 people cheered them on! How did they get there, and how and when did they ever get home, no one will ever know, but there was a tremendous show of boots, galoshes, earmuffs, skis and ski clothing, that showed that more than 15,000 people made it on foot. It is almost incidental that Riggs, that great money player, won this first and most important match of the tour in four sets, for Kramer suffered somewhat from "opening night jitters" and didn't play his best. The real point was that like so many other episodes in Riggs's career, in itself it was a unique event.

Bobby was always a gambler, a hustler, and a showman. He reveled in setting up freak matches at tennis, which would entice a player to bet on himself against Bobby. He would play someone while wearing a heavy raccoon fur coat and carrying a bucket of water in his nonracquet hand, and he dreamed up a number of other outrageous propositions to lure bets out of innocent "pigeons." An excellent golfer, he did the same sort of thing on the golf course, and Bobby was

such a good competitor that he won a huge majority of these fantastic
propositions. Therefore, after having enjoyed a very considerable number of years as a champion senior tennis player, it was quite in character for Bobby to conceive the biggest ballyhoo event in tennis history, the "Battle of the Sexes," in 1973.

Riggs, fifty-five years old by then, orchestrated and promoted the whole thing. He billed himself as the country's No. 1 Male Chauvenist Pig and declared that a man like himself, with one foot in the grave so to speak, could still beat the best women tennis players in the world. He challenged Margaret Smith Court, one of the only two women who ever won the Grand Slam, a previous winner of the Wimbledon title on three occasions and the U.S. National championship four times, and still so much at the peak of her game that, later in this same year of 1973, she took the U.S. championship once again. The match was to be played in May, on Mothers' Day, and a fantastic promotion campaign was staged, with so much interest being worked up that CBS bought television rights to show the match live, despite the fact that it was obviously no real match of players of different sexes and comparable standing. Riggs was some thirty years past his prime while she was still in hers, but Riggs went into rigorous training, was in great shape, and utterly destroyed a very nervous Margaret Court, who took the burden of representing feminism too seriously and didn't do herself justice at all. Riggs won, 6–2, 6–1, which seemed to confirm Male Chauvenist Pig boasts. Actually, the match didn't prove a thing except that Riggs could still play pretty darned good tennis, despite his age, and Court, who everyone knew played as well as any woman in the world, was wiped out by the pressures the occasion engendered for her. (If you are interested and don't know, in no sport can a woman compete successfully against a man of equal standing and talent, and tennis is no exception, although the gap may be closing since the day in the 1920s when Suzanne Lenglen thought she could give Bill Tilden a game, and challenged him to play a set. She didn't win more than a few points, losing 6–0, and they were the unchallenged champions of their respective sexes at that time. And even today Chris Evert says that her brother, who isn't ranked at all, beats her. Men simply have too much of a physical edge for a woman to overcome it, and that's the only reason. A great woman champion may have just as good an arsenal of shots, and just as keen a knowledge of tactics as a great male champion, but his power and stride and speed make a competitive match unfair.)

Well, that is beside the point in the 1973 Battle of the Sexes, the second act of which engendered even greater fanfare than the first. This time Riggs was to face Billie Jean King, then current Wimbledon champion and the other top woman player of the time, in a match set for September in the Houston Astrodome. This time ABC purchased the right to televise the event in prime time, no less, and there were all sorts of juicy commercial tie-ins. The biggest crowd in tennis history witnessed the event, 30,472, and millions saw the television coverage. Riggs had been paying much more attention to staging the affair than he had to training or practicing, and while he put on an extravaganza of a stage exhibition that night that rivaled the Ziegfield Follies, he then played very poorly. Mrs. King, a belligerent battler for women's rights and a cool customer when the chips were down, took the encounter seriously and played superlative tennis. She won soundly in straight sets, 6–4, 6–3, 6–3, which made a nice finish to the fairly foolish Battles, since each sex won once and lost once.

Nothing much was proved by all this except that everybody concerned made a great deal of money.

BUD COLLINS

There is no middle ground when tennis fans start rating the announcers who cover the game on television—at least not as far as Bud Collins is concerned. You either love him or hate him, but the haters are in a very small minority and the things about him that enrage them haven't anything to do with the unquestioned knowledge and authority he brings to tennis coverage on TV. These misanthropes are simply furious because Bud has a wild sense of humor and can be caustically funny about certain establishment figures, but even more they are disconcerted by the flamboyant attire he chooses to wear. Nothing like some of his shirts and ties has been seen this side of Hawaii, and as for some multicolored patterned pants he's acquired somewhere, the only word for them is outrageous. So Bud does come across pretty loudly on color television, as far as the visuals are concerned, and he is very voluble on the audio side as well, but anyone who gets annoyed enough with Bud's discourses to turn off the sound not only has no sense of humor, but also is probably not a very astute tennis spectator.

For Bud Collins knows the game thoroughly, loves it intensely, and shares his exhuberance with the viewer in a highly amusing and even sophisticated style. But he doesn't take tennis or his role overly seriously. Once when a man wrote him that whenever Bud was broadcasting, he turned on Mozart and turned Bud off, Collins responded: "You are a man of discriminating taste. I wish I could do the same." And any time somebody implies that he ought to be fired, Collins says "you're entitled." He figures he will be fired some day, because he's a public figure of sorts, like a baseball manager, and they all get fired. He says, "If Edward R. Murrow could get fired, I think Bud Collins can too."

Tennis on television will be the poorer, however, when and if that

Taylor Jones

ever happens, for Bud Collins lights up what is frequently a dreary
scene with his inventive images and vocabulary. One of the most
dreary recent scenes took place in the last French Open, when two
accomplished topspin specialists, Ivan Lendl and Mats Wilander, both
decided to try to outlast the other, with the result that the ball traveled
safely back and forth across the net eighty-three times on one point,
with neither player ever trying to advance to the net, or even hit out
forcefully in an attempt to put the ball away. Bud moodily watched this
performance and others like it, and explained that the red clay surface,
on which the French Open is contested, encouraged the use of such
tactics, but after a while he modestly observed that if this kept up, the
game of tennis was in grave danger of contracting "terminal topspin."

That was a typical Bud Collinsism, a piece of humorous but
pertinent imagery that seems to be his to command at will. Two other
examples are "bagel" and "Cyclops," both of which you will find in the
Lexicon. Sometimes Bud will not claim credit for coining a word or
phrase that sounds as if he surely had conceived it, but he adopts it
and uses it to more telling effect than anyone else. That would be the
case with "Lingering Death" and "hacker." With respect to the latter,
Bud calls himself a hacker, but he does himself an injustice. He is a
very good tennis player indeed, a top club-level performer, and he has
one characteristic about his game that truly sets him apart. Whenever
and wherever it's allowed, Bud likes to play bare-footed! That's a
preference that may be understandable if the surface is grass, but Bud
makes no distinctions. A sun-baked, red-hot hard surface, or a
groundkeeper's injunction, may force Bud to don tennis shoes, but it
takes that sort of thing to make him do so.

Bud Collins's original job in sports was a rookie reporter on *The
Boston Herald*, and the worst assignment you could get in those days
was to cover tennis. The sports editor who sent him out on his first
assignment, covering the Massachusetts State Ladies championships,
actually apologized to Bud for having to do so, but Collins, an avid
tennis player himself, fell in love with the work right away and has
never stopped being in love with it. Today he is a staff member and
columnist of *The Boston Globe*, and does the tennis commentary for
NBC's television coverage of the French Open, and Wimbledon. He

says that if you're committed to a career of sports coverage, it's a nice job. "You don't have to work for a living; you sit outdoors in nice places like Roland Garros and Wimbledon. As a newspaperman, I've covered almost everything, and being in Paris or London beats being in Kansas City with the Boston Red Sox."

Collins has a special affection for Rod Laver, on whose autobiography, *The Education of a Tennis Player*, he collaborated, which is a polite way of saying he was the ghost writer. The book came out at the height of Laver's fame, shortly after Laver completed his second Grand Slam, and Laver and he became fast friends at that time and have remained so.

In an interview with Tom Tebbutt in *Tennis Week*, Collins told an amusing story about a particular experience with another player:

"I used to write and talk on TV about Betty Stove as 'Big Bad Betty.' I meant it as a compliment but she didn't like it and told me never to call her that. In the American idiom at the time it was like 'Bad, Bad Leroy Brown.' After the next time I called her Big Bad Betty on TV, she came up to me in Palm Springs and put out her hand to shake hands and flipped me right over her back and said, 'Don't call me Big Bad Betty.' I said, 'Never again.'

MAUREEN CONNOLLY

In her autobiography, *Chrissie*, Chris Evert tells about the day in 1981 when she and Hana Mandlikova were sitting in the Players' Waiting Room at Wimbledon, preparatory to their going out onto Centre Court for their singles final match. Hana was looking at the photographs on the wall, and when she came to one that bore the name Maureen Connolly in elegant letters underneath it, she turned to Chris and inquired, "Who's that?" Hana had never heard of her.

Admittedly Mandlikova was only nineteen years old at the time, Connolly's fame was some thirty years earlier, and history is usually not the favorite subject of the young. Foreign born, one might not have expected her to know anything about bygone American heroes, but tennis was Mandlikova's life, career, and bread and butter, and it did seem surprising that the name of one of her most illustrious predecessors meant nothing to her.

For Little Mo Connolly had such a brilliant tennis career that, in the all too few years that Fate allotted her before a tragic accident cut it short, she brought the spectators at Forest Hills and at Wimbledon out to see her, rather than the men players. At the time—the early 1950s—women's tennis held little attraction. The great match between Suzanne Lenglen and Helen Wills, a quarter of a century earlier (see article) had attracted world-wide interest, but since then attendance at the women's championships and the Wightman Cup matches had drawn such pitifully small galleries that the championships were combined with the men's tournament, and the Wightman matches transferred to smaller clubs.

Maureen Connolly changed all that and became the biggest drawing card in the tennis world. When only sixteen, she became the youngest player up to that time—1951—ever to win the U.S. National women's title, and then went on to be the youngest winner in Wimbledon

115

history as well. She won each of these two greatest of tournaments **117**
three times in succession. In only three years she won a unique
sequence of nine major world championships — before she was
twenty—including becoming the first woman ever to achieve the
Grand Slam. Between September 1951 and July 1954 she was never
beaten anywhere in the world, except once in one minor tournament
in California, and she almost never lost even a set while doing so. The
severity of her drives, both forehand and backhand, reminded old-
timers of the immortal Helen Wills, while the subtleties of her lobs and
drop shots, and her unquenchable spirit that enabled her to pull out
tough matches, were without equal. The only parts of her arsenal that
were not superb, her service and her volleying, were more than
adequate. They must have been because nobody could beat Little
Mo. Had she been able to play another decade or more past the age of
twenty, as most fine players do, there is little doubt that she would
have polished and strengthened whatever minor weaknesses she may
have had in her game, and might well have rung up an unparalleled
number of major championships. No one ever was more firmly
established on the road to such a record.

However, a few months before she seemed a sure thing to win her
fourth consecutive National title at Forest Hills, Miss Connolly, a most
enthusiastic and accomplished equestrienne, was riding when her
horse took fright and whirled into a cement-mixer truck in San Diego.
She sustained so serious a fracture of her leg that not only could she
not defend her U.S. title, but had to give up competitive tennis
permanently.

All this was, of course, long before the modern era in which such
players as Billie Jean King and Chris Evert and Martina Navratilova
(and now Steffi Graf) would have to be considered in an all-time
ranking of the best women players who ever lived, but back then two
very authoritative attempts were made, one by American George Lott,
and the other by Britisher Peter Wilson. Lott ranked Helen Wills
Moody No. 1, Maureen Connolly No. 2, and Suzanne Lenglen No. 3.
Wilson ranked Lenglen 1, Connolly 2, and Mrs. Moody 3. To rate this
slip of a girl, with only three years of world competition behind her, as
a peer of the two former goddesses of tennis would seem to be

enough to inspire Hana Mandlikova to learn something about Maureen Connolly, but there's even more. Both Lott and Wilson agree that, had she been able to enjoy a full tennis career, Little Mo would probably have to be rated the best of all.

The Connolly saga ends on the saddest note of all. In 1969 Maureen Connolly Brinker, age thirty-four, died of cancer. A foundation in her name was established in Dallas, Texas, where the Brinkers lived.

FRANK KOVACS

He was called the Clown Prince of Tennis, and the sobriquet had a double meaning. The Prince part was meaningful because he was always on the threshhold of being the best player in the world in the years just before the United States entered World War II, but he never quite made it, chiefly because he was a contemporary of Bobby Riggs at his peak, and when Riggs was at his peak, nobody was beating him. In fact, Don Budge once called Kovacs "the greatest player in the world who never won a big tournament."

There were reasons for that, and one of them was simple laziness, or at least unwillingness to buckle down to hard work at tennis. Bill Tilden wrote that great champions are not born but are made by their own—and at times their coaches'— efforts. He wrote that he had yet to find a born tennis player, and the best he had been able to do was to find a gifted athlete, but only long, hard work made the player. The two greatest naturals he ever saw were Vincent Richards and Frank Kovacs but (Tilden wrote) neither had quite the willingness to do the long serious practice work that produces a champion of champions and an all-time great.

The other reason why Frank never reached the heights in tennis of which he was capable has to do with the Clown portion of his title. He was truly a clown, the most spontaneously inventive and endearing prankster who ever played major tennis. He simply didn't take himself, or tennis, very seriously. He wasn't a bad actor on a tennis court, not in the way that Ilie Nastase and Jimmy Connors and John McEnroe have been on occasion. Kovacs did unorthodox things during a match that disturbed opponents and infuriated officials, but it was all in good fun, and not motivated by spleen or contempt. He would hit balls behind his back and between his legs. Playing in the quarterfinals of the 1940 National championships against Joe Hunt, he felt weary and stale

after having played in twenty consecutive tournaments. He had no heart for the match, had already reserved space on a California-bound plane that night, and had decided just to go through the motions against Hunt, and then take off. However, being Kovacs, he decided to enjoy things while he was still around, so after fooling away the first two sets, he really started clowning in the third. He tossed up three balls simultaneously on a service and blasted the middle one over for an ace. After a while, Hunt called for a halt and asked the umpire to make Kovacs stop clowning, but Kovacs replied that he always enjoyed winning, and now he insisted upon enjoying losing. Hunt refused to go on, so then Kovacs sat down in the middle of the court, and strummed his racquet as if it were a guitar. Hunt too sat down on the baseline opposite, while countless officials sprang up from everywhere, plead-ing, cajoling, and threatening Frank, who remained firm about his sit-down strike while Hunt fumed, and the gallery went off into paroxyms of mirth. After a full quarter of an hour, Hunt was persuaded to stand up and continue the match no matter what lunacy Kovacs might yet have in mind, so he did, and quickly ran out the set, knocking Kovacs out of the tournament but allowing him to catch his plane. Despite this, at the end of the year Kovacs was ranked No. 3 in the nation, while Joe Hunt was ranked No. 5.

Two years before that, once again in the National championships at Forest Hills, Frank was matched against Vic Seixas on a sweleringly hot day. Male tennis players back then still had to wear the traditional long flannel trousers in major tournaments like Forest Hills and Wimbledon, but the match was very closely contested and the heat was intolerable for the players. Suddenly, in the middle of the fifth and deciding set, Kovacs produced a pair of scissors from somewhere and lopped his pants off some two feet, so that they only came down to a point a few inches above his knees. Bunny Austin is credited with being the first prominent tennis player to adopt shorts, and put them across so that they were recognized as legitimate tennis apparel, but perhaps Frank Kovacs deserves to be mentioned too.

In 1941, Kovacs attained his highest ranking, No. 2 to Bobby Riggs, to whom he lost in the final at Forest Hills. His backhand was superb, and his standard greeting to Don Budge, whose backhand was universally conceded to be the best ever seen, was "Hello, Don. How's the second best backhand in the world coming?" Admittedly, he heckled umpires and linesmen in a fashion that had never been seen before on the staid courts of Forest Hills and elsewhere, but it was always obvious that he was clowning around, both for his own benefit and the enjoyment of the gallery, and there was no venom in his antics. He was immensely popular, not only with other players but also with the spectators and the press. Of course it didn't hurt that he was extremely good looking, and the bobby soxers adored him.

Frank was justly known as a charming screwball when he was cavorting around the tennis world, and when he went off to join the army in World War II, he reported to his basic training camp carrying along a set of golf clubs and a ukelele, but the war was more serious business for him than what had gone before, and he settled down to work. From buck private he worked his way up to lieutenant, and served with distinction in the South Pacific, before returning to his native California, where he taught Tennis-with-a-Smile for many years.

JAMES VAN ALEN

Jimmy Van Alen is in his mid-eighties now, but no one would ever think of him as embodying anything other than the Spirit of Eternal Youth. Apart from his appearance at Newport Casino social and tennis affairs, invariably attired in a wide-brimmed planter's straw hat, a striped tie bearing the Casino's colors, beige slacks, and suede shoes, he still is the wildly imaginative, energetic character who has originated and carried out a number of projects that originally seemed impossible.

It wasn't long after he graduated from Cambridge University, in England, that Jimmy, not only a major letter winner there at tennis, but also a fantastically good and enthusiastic player of court tennis, the ancient royal game, hit upon the idea of forming an American team to play an international match of court tennis against a combined Oxford-Cambridge team. Both British universities had facilities in which to play the game, but there were practically no such courts in the United States at all, and certainly none at any college. Van Alen picked out the best squash racquets players at Yale, Harvard, and Princeton, and arranged for them to learn the game and to play on the few facilities that existed at the Racquet Clubs of New York, Boston, and Philadelphia. Within the year the Americans became good enough that Van Alen was able to stage his international match very successfully.

Jimmy was a fourth-generation resident of Newport, the site of our National championships from the very first one in 1881 through 1914, after which the tournament was moved to Forest Hills. For years the idea of a Tennis Hall of Fame had been kicked around, but nobody ever did anything about it. Van Alen not only put the idea across and into being in 1954, but had it set up in the Newport Casino, which he dominated like the tennis royalty he is. On top of

that he persuaded enough Casino stockholders to donate their shares to the Hall of Fame that the Hall got overwhelming control of the Casino and so assured itself both of its growth and a permanent home.

It has been in later years, however, that Van Alen's major contributions to the game of tennis almost caused revolutions. Yet it now seems indisputable that everyone, from players through spectators to the television networks, are immensely grateful that Van Alen thought too many tennis matches were interminably long marathons, and something should be done to streamline them. His first attempt, in the early 1960s, was to introduce VASSS— the Van Alen Simplified Scoring System. This used the scoring system of table tennis, but with thirty-one points winning a game (and match), and made it possible to control the length of a match within reasonable limits. There would be no matches enduring for several hours, which seemed a blessing not only for the players but also for spectators who wanted to see a variety of matches in a tournament, rather than one or two almost unending affairs. It also seemed tailor-made for the television people, who could schedule important matches without having the strong possibility that they'd either have to cut a match short before its conclusion, or sacrifice some very popular feature scheduled to follow the tennis.

But the tennis world almost laughed Van Alen off the globe when he tried to introduce VASSS, and despite his bulldog quality of never quitting in a fight, he wasn't getting anywhere. Well, he finally decided to put on his own tournament at Newport Casino, and offered enough cash prizes to lure the best professionals to have a stab at a VASSS tournament, even though they were distrustful of the scoring and hated another embellishment Jimmy added—that a service line be drawn three feet behind the baseline to cut down the advantage for net-rushers. He rigged up banks of lights for night play, and was able to put on ten matches a day (in afternoon and evening sessions) under a round-robin system that gave the spectators a chance to see *every player* in action *each day*. The spectators loved it, but at the beginning the pros were not so keen. Losers complained to the skies, the loudest being Pancho Gonzales, who never did stop complaining. Rod Laver didn't like it either until he found he could win in the end anyway, as he did, winning the tournament handily after he has lost his very first match to a lesser pro whom he had always beaten. Everybody who saw Van Alen's VASSS affair went quite wild about it, but he couldn't put it across with the tennis establishment, so he started working on something else that might suit the big-wigs better, and still achieve his goal—to bring about a foreseeable end to tennis matches that go on forever. He invented Sudden Death (see Lexicon), a way to end things quickly when any set reaches 6–6, and it was adopted both for the Wimbledon tournament and the Forest Hills one, and it won converts almost immediately among the galleries. A red flag was put up at each court whenever a Sudden Death situation loomed, and everybody rushed over to see it. It added a new excitement to tennis that was irresistible.

The players resisted it, to some extent, however. Many felt keenly that a set (and sometimes it would be an entire match) shouldn't rest upon the result of one point, which could be the case in Sudden Death. So a more complicated version of Van Alen's brainstorm was devised, the tiebreaker, or Lingering Death (see Lexicon), which embodies the same general idea but which doesn't end quite so abruptly. Jimmy thought it was a mistake and continued to favor his original idea, but a vote among the players decided the issue, and the tiebreaker is now the accepted rule in all the big tournaments. Even though he didn't work that alternative out, it is clearly based upon Jimmy's concept, and it never would have come into being without Van Alen's brilliance and tenacity.

Jimmy also developed the No-Ad scoring system (see Lexicon), another way of shortening tennis matches, and this has been used in National intercollegiate play since 1972, and is also a favorite for many club tournaments.

BORIS BECKER & STEFFI GRAF

Not since those memorable days back in 1974 when Jimmy Connors and Chris Evert truly arrived on the scene in a big way at the same time, each winning both the Wimbledon and the United States singles titles of their respective sexes, have two players done anything like it again. But in 1985 a young man, Boris Becker, and a young woman, Steffi Graf, both West Germans, both extremely young, and both virtually unknown, created a comparable impact upon a tennis world that, for certain reasons, had become rather jaded as far as interest in the best players was concerned. Becker and Graf revitalized the game.

Everything about them was fresh, surprising, and intriguing. For one thing, Germany wasn't known as a tennis nation, or at least it hadn't been known as one for half a century, since Baron Gottfried von Cramm had his memorable battles against Donald Budge, and Cecile (Cilly) Aussem had surprisingly won the 1931 Wimbledon ladies' title, beating another German woman, Hilda Krahwinkel, in the final. Henner Henkel had been a staunch teammate of von Cramm in 1937 when Germany almost won the Davis Cup, and about in the same era Hans Nusslein had been regarded by experts as being every bit as good as von Cramm, but Nusslein was always a professional and so could not play in the amateur tournaments that, at that time, were the only way a person could win recognition and world ranking. Except for Wilhelm Bungert, who was a good player some years later, that just about ends the list of German players of whom anybody ever heard until Boris Becker and Steffi Graf suddenly popped up, unless (and this is purely for trivia fans, because she never made a dent in

big-time tennis) you want to include Angelique Pfannenberg. She played tennis, but she is remembered because she married the great Australian champion John Newcombe.

Becker was the first of the two young stars to leap into the spotlight in 1985, and he did it in the most spectacular way possible. In the Stella Artois tournament at the Queens Club in London, which is played on grass a couple of weeks before Wimbledon and is the best guideline to what's likely to happen at Wimbledon, Becker unexpectedly demolished all the opposition and won the event. Few were really convinced that he would do the same a fortnight later at Wimbledon, and he was not the odds-makers' favorite to win. In fact, he was not even seeded. But win he did, and from that moment on, Becker has had to be considered a good bet against anyone else in the world. Still, the challenge of being able to repeat his Wimbledon triumph the following year, with players like Ivan Lendl and the great Swedes in the field, seemed too much to expect from someone who in 1986 was still only eighteen. Besides that, Becker did seem to be something of a peak-and-valley player. He would beat the best in the world in three successive tournaments, and then lose to a fairly undistinguished Spanish player, Sergio Casal, in an important Davis Cup match. But when that most important tournament of all, Wimbledon, rolled around again, Becker was more than ready for it, and he swept through the field again, to become the greatest idol in his country. An unbelievable 98 percent of West Germans know his name and hold him in higher esteem than anyone else in the nation, and when he loses—and lose he sometimes does—criticism of him is deemed almost unpatriotic.

Becker had convinced the tennis world that Wimbledon was his turf, so to speak, so by the time his third tournament there opened, in June 1987, he was almost a prohibitive favorite to defend his title successfully. This was despite the fact that 1987 had been a strange, emotional, and fitful year for him up to that time. He had a prolonged fit of temper, berating officials and breaking three racquets, in a losing match in the Australian Open, and his penitence about it didn't quite erase the memory. He fell out with, and let go, his coach of many years, Gunther Bosch, preferring the less demanding overseeing of his

130 career by Ion Tiriac. He found romance with Mademoiselle Benedicte Coutin of Monaco, and she became his regular traveling companion. In other words, in a little over one year's time, Becker, as Tiriac put it, "lived a lifetime. He was a sheltered boy and now he is a human being who makes his own decisions, and making those decisions is the important thing for him." Becker agrees with this assessment, considers 1987 his happiest year, and feels that Tiriac is a real friend under whose hands-off guidance he can flourish. So it was a shock when, in one of the most spectacular upsets in Wimbledon history, Boris was eliminated in his very first match by a completely unknown Australian player, Peter Doohan, who was soon put out of the running himself. The fact that it was Wimbledon, and Becker was such an outstanding favorite, made it particularly shocking, but perhaps it should not have been. Surely the pressure on Becker was intense, and even in lesser events he has been known to lose unexpectedly. The reason is that so much is expected of him, because his triumphs have been so notable, and also because he is a player who goes out and takes unusual risks in an effort to win every point. When it works, he's unbeatable. When it doesn't work, a Peter Doohan wins a day's big headlines, which is nice for him even if it throws all of West Germany into a trough of despair.

The other West German luminary, Steffi Graf, first won her spurs in a big way in the quarterfinal round of the 1985 U.S. Open at Flushing Meadow, with a victory that didn't set too well with the American crowd. She was only fifteen years old then, and she seemed to be just a determined, not very appealing little girl, who was giving all sorts of trouble to the extremely attractive and popular American player, Pam Shriver, who was one of the country's top-ranking women stars. Shriver had a brilliant all-court game, and went up to net at every opportunity, and it was unbelievable how this undersized child was able to counter her efforts usually by blasting a scorching forehand from her deep court right past the desparately lunging Shriver at net. She didn't have much of a backhand—it was a conservative slice—but she never made an error off it and she didn't have to use it too often, because whenever she could she ran around it and took Pam's shot on that deadly forehand. (Bud Collins dubbed her Fraulein Forehand.) It was truly the match of the women's tournament that year, and Steffi pulled it out in the end, just as she's been doing ever since in tight matches almost without exception.

Graf gave the Americans an even more startling show the following year at the U.S. Open when, for one of the few times in her short career to date, she lost a nip-and-tuck match. It was certainly forgivable, for she was meeting the then unbeatable champion, Martina Navratilova, and she had her match point three times, before finally succumbing, and actually suffering something of a bad break in the process. Never mind. With this match Steffi Graf proved that she belonged in the same class as Martina and Chris Evert, the two who had dominated women's tennis for so long that tournaments had become dull, until the inevitable meeting of Martina and Chris in the final.

After that defeat, despite a siege of illness that prevented her playing at Wimbledon, Steffi went on to win seven tournaments in a row, including the French Open where she beat Martina, and forty-five matches in a row before Martina finally turned the tables in Wimbledon and the U.S. Open in 1987.

But Steffi Graf is here to stay, and with Chris thinking of retirement, and Martina not getting any younger, she bids fair to be the next dominant champion, with only the erratic Hana Mandlikova and the even younger, but extremely promising Argentine beauty, Gabriella Sabatini, seeming to be real threats. Steffi brought to women's tennis what Boris Becker brought to men's—a young new face and an exciting and flamboyant game, just when the scene in both men's and women's tennis had turned somewhat flat.

Taylor Jones

ROD LAVER

It's hard to believe that Rodney George Laver, the Rocket, will turn fifty in August 1988, but if you met him today and hadn't been counting, the chances are you wouldn't know it. He looks very much the same as he did through his twenties and early thirties when he dominated the world of men's tennis. It's true that the once carrot-colored thatch of hair has picked up quite a lot of gray, but that's about the only difference, and on a tennis court, that wouldn't be likely to be noticeable, for Rod has invariably favored playing in a crinkled, white tennis hat that, in hot weather, he lines with wet cabbage leaves. "Keeps a bloke cool," he explains.

All the other physical characteristics of this native Australian, who has made his home in California for many years, haven't changed much. He is still the left-handed, bow-legged, liberally freckled chap whose 5 foot, 8 inch frame still doesn't tip the beam on the scales at more than 150 pounds, and even though he now plays with the seniors, he still can run all day and belt the life out of a tennis ball with that left forearm. Dave Anderson, of the *New York Times*, once persuaded the Rocket to allow him to measure that forearm and wrist with a tape measure, and it turned out that the forearm was 12 inches around and the wrist 7 inches around, both bigger than the comparable measurements of the heavyweight champion of the era. Yes, if you had seen Laver playing in the 1960s and early 1970s, you'd have no trouble recognizing him today, especially if you also saw Paul Hogan in the movie, "Crocodile Dundee," because a lot of talented Australians seem to look remarkably alike.

Rod grew up in Rockhampton, in Queensland, Australia, the son of a keenly enthusiastic father who built an ant-bed tennis court for his son to play on when he was thirteen years old and showed a lot of promise. That was, and is, quite a common type of court in Australia, for materials are plentiful and the labor of digging out one of the huge red ant hills, crushing it, and then spreading it onto level ground with the grass scraped off and rolling it in, is all. Once that's done you have one of the best dirt-type surfaces in the world—it plays a lot like clay. Laver and his brothers had been playing with their parents before then, but a professional, Charlie Hollis, told Mr. Laver that Rodney, the smallest and youngest of the boys, was the one who really showed promise. He took him in hand before eventually turning him over to Harry Hopman, the tennis professional who was responsible for developing all the many magnificant Australian champions who really ruled world tennis, with very few interruptions, from 1950 to 1970. Hopman is given credit for much of the success of a couple of dozen Australians who won the Wimbledon or U. S. championships or both, including such immortals as Frank Sedgman, Lew Hoad, Ken Rosewall, John Newcombe, Ashley Cooper, Neale Fraser, Roy Emerson, and Tony Roche, but Rod Laver was the greatest of them all.

It's doubtful if any player in history ever reached such a concentrated and sustained peak of domination over his peers as Laver did during the several-weeks duration of the Tennis Champions Classic of 1971. The Open tournaments had been established, so all of the top players had now turned professional, and the richest cash prize ever offered for tennis up to that time had been posted for this event— $210,000. (That seems like pin money in comparison with what's at stake today, but it was a whopping sum for tennis back then.)

A hand-picked field of the greatest tennis players in the world were to meet each other, head to head, every few days, for $10,000 on a winner-take-all basis, with each winner moving on to face a new challenger in a different city. When you have players of this caliber meeting each other often, one player may emerge having won a substantial majority of matches, but it seemed inconceivable that anyone could do what Rod Laver did. He won every single match out of the sixteen he had to play, and picked up all the money it was possible for one player to win— $160,000. When you consider that the field included such stars as Rosewall, Newcombe, Emerson, Arthur Ashe, and others of comparable stature, Laver's run of sixteen

successive triumphs must rank high among the most spectacular feats
in tennis history.

Of course, by 1971, people had come to expect almost any miracle from the all-conquering strings of Laver's racquet. As an amateur he had been the only male player since Don Budge to sweep all four of the major tournaments, and so win the Grand Slam. He might well have done it several more times if he had been allowed to enter those events, but they were for amateurs, and after his Grand Slam achievement, Laver turned professional. However, when the great tournaments finally became Opens in 1968, and professionals were eligible, Laver once again waltzed through the Australian, French, Wimbledon, and Forest Hills tournaments to achieve what no one else has ever done, a second Grand Slam, in 1969. That was, of course, an even greater triumph than the first, because every fine player in the world was eligible to play, whether amateur or professional.

A good case could be made that the Rocket was the best player the game has ever seen, Bill Tilden not excluded, but as in all sports, that's a discussion that can never be settled one way or the other, for times, conditions, and circumstances make direct comparisons between the heroes of one generation with another a bootless endeavor. Let's leave it that he certainly deserves to be mentioned in the same breath with Tilden.

Taylor Jones

CHRIS EVERT & MARTINA NAVRATILOVA

When tennis histories are written in the next generation, the names of Chris Evert and Martina Navratilova will surely be linked, for theirs has been a personal rivalry almost unmatched in great sports legends. Suzanne Lenglen and Helen Wills only met on the tennis court on one occasion and yet one thinks of them together because of the drama surrounding that single encounter. But Chris and Martina have faced each other almost eighty times during the decade from 1978 through 1987 when one or the other ruled the world of women's tennis, and no long-lived competition could possibly have been more intense, although it has been softened to some extent in recent years by a bond of genuine respect and friendship. This is despite the fact that their backgrounds, temperaments, and personal lives could hardly be more dissimilar.

Few American athletes of either sex have ever projected so wholesome and altogether attractive an image as Chris Evert has done ever since she first burst on the scene as a talented teenager in pigtails. As she matured and became the No. 1 player in the world in 1974 (a ranking she repeated in 1975, 1976, 1977, 1980, and 1981), she displayed admirable character as well as formidable athletic tenacity, and no breath of criticism was ever leveled against her as she set a host of modern-day records: most Grand Slam singles titles (18); most singles titles (152); and most career match victories (more than 1200). Invariably gracious in victory and equally so in defeat when Martina, a few years younger, finally caught up to her and started to beat her, Chris has been the darling of every tennis fan who appreciates her qualities that combine tenacity on the court with grace on it and off.

Who was the No. 1 player in the world in those years that are missing from the list above? Martina Navratilova, of course, who had been chasing Chris but had lost twenty out of twenty-four matches to her prior to 1978. Then she finally caught up and passed her, beating her for the Wimbledon title, Martina's first of the eight she has now won. That was the turning point in their rivalry, for though Evert still held the edge in matches won through 1980, 30–18, Navratilova had been rated the world's best in 1978 and 1979. Chris regained her position at the top in 1980 and 1981, as noted above, but ever since then Martina has enjoyed a clear edge, including thirteen straight victories over Chris in 1983 and 1984 on her way to dominating women's tennis solidly for the half dozen years from 1982 through 1987. (In that final year Steffi Graf, with more victories, could lay claim to having been No. 1, but Navratilova won both Wimbledon and the U. S. Open, which are the two tournaments that really matter.)

Martina Navratilova was a Czechoslovakian who, by the time she was emerging from her teens, had already defected and become an American citizen, as well as one of the world's best women players. She was an exhuberant young woman who fell in love immediately with all things American, including junk food, and since she already tilted the beams a little too much on the heavy side, she threatened to balloon up and then out of top-level tennis. That didn't turn out to be the case, however, and Martina took herself and her appetite in hand and, beginning around 1975, started beating everybody except Chris Evert pretty regularly. Martina played a very flashy, aggressive game, storming the net and volleying like the best men players, which was quite a contrast to the powerful but always steady sharpshooting from the backcourt that Evert used to subdue all opponents, including brash net-rushers like Navratilova. But three years later the story was different. Evert was as good as ever, and could raise her game frequently to battle Navratilova all the way in important matches, and even win some of them, but Martina won more. At the end of 1985 their series was tied at thirty-one matches won for each: today Martina enjoys about a five-match edge.

Doubles partners for a while when Martina was very young, they split in 1975 when the singles rivalry was beginning to get intense, but Chris and Martina have always gotten on well and are respectful of each other. Their friendship may be stronger today than it ever was, despite their private lives away from tennis being about as different as any two women's could be. Chris, with her calm, unruffled, and generally unemotional court demeanor, was once labeled by sports-writers The Ice Maiden. It was not an apt nickname for a very warm-blooded young woman who had a much-publicized teenage romance with Jimmy Connors that seemed for a while to be leading towards marriage. Later her marriage to Britisher John Lloyd survived some periods of separation before the Lloyds finally became divorced, and during that time it was pretty well known that Chris was involved with other men. Chris was and is essentially a private person, but in recent years she does not seem to have minded her image changing from the little innocent that she was once regarded as being, to a more worldly and sophisticated one. Currently she is traveling the circuit quite openly with former U.S. Olympic skier Andy Mill. In press conferences she gracefully reserves her right to privacy and turns aside too much prying, but she says that she's outgrown the All-American Girl image that was thrust upon her as a youngster, and now she wants to be herself.

Martina, on the other hand, appears always to have been herself in never having been involved with men, and frankly admitting that her romantic attachments have been with women. Her honesty in this respect seems characteristic of what we see on the court where, although she keeps her emotions tightly in check and is never anything other than the most exemplary of sportswomen, there doesn't seem to be any subtlety or concealment of how things are with her at that particular moment. Honesty is a characteristic one associ-ates with Martina's performance on the tennis court, and she has never been anything but open and frank about her private life.

After a decade during which the criticism of women's tennis has been that it's largely been confined to Evert and Navratilova, with lamentably few challenges from anyone else, a new wave of young players is coming to the fore and threatening to take over in the next few years. Steffi Graf has done more than threaten. She is already at the top, and players like Gabriella Sabatini and Lori McNeil and others seem likely soon to be up there challenging too. Yet it may be a long time before we again see the likes of two such superstars as Chris and Martina, waging such a long series of unparalleled brilliance against each other with such determination but always with the highest code of sportsmanship.

INDEX